The Ancient Slavs

THE ANCIENT SLAVS

Settlement and Society

The Rhind Lectures 1989–90

MARTIN GOJDA

EDINBURGH UNIVERSITY PRESS

© M. Gojda 1991
Edinburgh University Press
22 George Square, Edinburgh

Set in Lasercomp Times Roman
by the Alden Press Ltd, London
and printed by Page Bros Ltd, Norwich.

British Library Cataloguing in Publication Data
Gojda, Martin
    The ancient Slavs: settlement and society.
    1. Slavonic civilization, history
    I. Title
    909.04918

    ISBN 0-7486-0200-3 (cased)

Contents

Foreword

In the 1989–90 session, the Rhind Lectures of the Society of Antiquaries of Scotland were delivered by Dr Martin Gojda, of the Archaeological Institute of the Czechoslovak Academy of Sciences, Prague. The lectures themselves had been instituted in 1876, through the benefaction of Alexander Henry Rhind of Wick, who wished to establish, through the Society, an annual course 'of not less than six lectures on some branch of archaeology, ethnology, ethnography, or allied topic'. Predominantly the lectures have been delivered by Insular, and especially by Scottish scholars. Rhind's own interests, however, had ranged widely over Europe and the Mediterranean; and appropriately, therefore, in several sessions the lectures have dealt with European archaeology.

So far as I can establish, however, none have been devoted to that major population group which stretches from the shores of the Black Sea to the Baltic region: namely, the Slavs. Even Professor Stuart Piggott's magisterial Rhind studies, *Ancient Europe* (Edinburgh University Press 1965), gives but a single line to the antecedents of the Slavs. Dr Gojda's lectures, on the settlement process of the ancient Slavs, therefore represent a major innovation. It may be of interest to explain the circumstances in which they came to be given.

I first met Martin Gojda at the World Archaeological Conference in Southampton in 1986. He was there as one of a group of Slav archaeologists, ranging in origin from Poland to the lower Danube, who were reading papers to the medieval sessions of the Congress. It was immediately apparent to a British medievalist that, despite individual national and political differences, the Slavs as a group presented what was virtually an alternative archaeology; or at least one that was radically different, in its concepts as well as its content, from that current in the west.

It seemed very worthwhile, therefore, to make this alternative archaeology accessible to English-language audiences. This has been attempted in two ways. The first was to publish in English the medieval papers delivered in Southampton, in a collection entitled *From the Baltic to the Black Sea: studies in medieval archaeology,* edited by David Austin and myself in the *One World Archaeology* series (Unwin Hyman 1990).

The second way to bring a characteristic sample of Slavic archaeology to a British audience was to use the opportunity offered by a prestigious lecture series in order to bring to this country one of the Slav scholars who had been at Southampton. Martin Gojda was an obvious choice, in terms both of his own scholarship and also his familiarity with Britain, including western Scotland, and his confidence in lecturing in English. As for a lecture platform, the Rhind series offered a highly suitable occasion. The Society of Antiquaries of Scotland is to be thanked for creating this opportunity; and Martin Gojda is to be congratulated on fulfilling it so admirably; and not least, by bringing his lectures so promptly to publication.

Dr Martin Gojda's own scenically-romantic city of Prague flanks the river Vltava, a river best known in the West as the theme of Smetana's great symphonic poem, *Die Moldau.* From the Slav heartland, the Vltava flows, not as we might expect, into the Baltic, nor into the Black Sea; but, as a tributary of the Elbe, it passes into the North Sea. It is a happy, if fanciful, thought that it ultimately mingles there with the Water of Leith, the river of Edinburgh where the lectures here published were originally delivered. What Martin Gojda took back to Prague was the undiluted gratitude and friendship of everyone who met him.

LESLIE ALCOCK

Preface

When, in 1987, on being asked by Prof. L. Alcock, the then President of the Society of Antiquaries of Scotland, to prepare a series of six lectures on the archaeology of the Slavs and to deliver them in Edinburgh as the Rhind Lectures, I was pleased that such an honour was conferred on me. Room was given with respect to individual lecture topics, implicitly allowing me to determine the overall orientation of the series. After discussion with Prof. Alcock, and taking my own experience with this sort of lecture into account, I concluded that a general introduction to the history and current stage of knowledge, of the origin and development of the Slavs and their historical process towards the state would be appropriate both for professionals and amateurs amongst the audience of the Rhind Lectures of 1989/90.

The lectures which follow are focused on some special problems of the early (and partly high) medieval settlement archaeology of Central and Eastern Europe. In the second lecture I will try to adumbrate the general trends in the settlement process of the Slavs. A survey of particular forms of this process (fortified centres and rural habitation sites) follows in the third and fourth lectures. An actual example of investigation of an early medieval rural site in the context of its environment, such as is demanded by the present needs of archaeology, is given in the fifth lecture, and the last lecture deals with the perspectives and objectives of settlement geography – an integral discipline studying patterns and systems of the human settlement process. Thus, the series proceeds from a general synthesis to the consideration of particular aspects which, with allowances made for the contexts of time and space, help to reveal the puzzle called history.

With regard to the limited range of the series it was impossible to incorporate, even in marginal notes, an outline of the cultural and religious manifestations of the ancient Slavs (architecture, decorative arts, ritual practice, ideology, etc.) which, strictly speaking, should not be omitted from the context of settlement process.

Owing to the fact that each lecture was prepared as an independent unit it was necessary, in a few cases, to repeat data which had been mentioned in previous lecture(s), thus making each lecture accessible to all, regardless of whether or not they had attended previous lectures.

A select bibliography is provided. As I consider this to be a basic informational survey and not strictly research work, I do not cite book and article references in the way common in scientific literature.

I believe that the international exchange of knowledge in ethno-historical processes helps to support relations among nations, even among those whose histories are not directly linked. This is what I consider to be the main objective of this lecture series.

List of Illustrations

1

The current state of settlement archaeology of the Slavs

The terms 'Slavic archaeology' or 'the archaeology of the (ancient) Slavs' were introduced into historical investigation around the turn of the nineteenth century. Until now it has been traditionally used as a designation for the discipline which is engaged in prospecting, collecting, elaborating, analysing and interpreting the remains of early medieval material culture derived from the vast territory which, since the Migration period, has been settled by Slavic ethnic groups. Although critical opinions on the validity of these terms occur sometimes in discussions or in journals it seems probable that in the future no changes will appear in this respect (in favour of, for instance, 'early medieval archaeology' or 'historical archaeology'). Incidentally, it is not an exclusively Eastern-European habit to label single archaeological disciplines after the nations which used to live in a territory during a certain period. Even in Britain the term 'Anglo-Saxon archaeology' or 'the archaeology of Anglo-Saxon England' has been frequently preferred over 'early medieval archaeology'. At this moment it should be stressed that the archaeology of the Slavs coincides, as regards the chronology, with the Anglo-Saxon period in England (C6–11 AD).

Slavic archaeology is traditionally considered a part of Slavic studies, a comprehensive scientific branch which, with the aid of many subdisciplines, studies the history and culture of Slavic nations. Stimulation to its development was given by the rise of the Enlightenment during the Age of Reason in eighteenth-century Europe. Through the effort of the so-called encyclo-paedists, history became a real scientific discipline which followed

1

not only political, but also social and economic reality in the nations' past. As well as this the rationalists gave birth to the term 'supranational history'; consequently, the instigation towards comprehensive Germanic, Romance, and Slavic studies was established.

The rise and rapid development of interest in the history of the Slavs can be seen in the countries in which the Slavic nations were incorporated in the multinational Hapsburg Monarchy and Hungarian State. With the coming of the Enlightenment at the end of eighteenth century, movements for the restoration of small European nations came into existence. This was known as National Revival. Having been suppressed by force, the Czech language and cultural tradition, for example, survived almost exclusively in the countryside as the language and culture of the low social classes in rural society and their extinction seemed to be inevitable. Thanks to favourable circumstances coming from abroad, influencing the thought and action of the top group of rulers in the Austrian confederation of states and nations, the possibility of the renaissance of the small European (Slavic) nations emerged. It was Johan Gottfried Herder (1744–1803), a German philosopher, whose ideas were accepted with true enthusiasm by Slavic patriots. In his work Herder gave credit to the role of the Slavs in European history (he called them 'Grecians of the New Age'). This was in connection with his espousal of the inalienable rights of each nation and his emphasis on the importance of a nation's language, tradition and folk culture.

In all probability Josef Dobrovský (1753–1829) was the person who established the concept of Slavic studies. Apart from his *History of Czech Language and Literature* and his *Introduction to the Old Slavic Language* written in German he was the author of the German/Czech dictionary. All these works influenced other scholars and gave impulse to further study of Czech language and culture. From the viewpoint of methodology, his appreciation of material (archaeological) sources was important to the future position of archaeology within historical studies. He was convinced that archaeological finds and features had full historical meaning and were of the same value as written documents. Thus, with this statement the discussion on what is the relation between archaeology and history started.

Hand in hand with linguistic study other disciplines come to the

1. Portrait of J. Dobrovský, the Czech founder of the Slavic studies.

fore. Of them the most important were ethnography and archaeology. Since the beginning they focused, in correspondence with the overall tendency of the National Revival, on the search for the ancient history of the Slavs; this effort was partly influenced by Romanticism, a widely spread philosophy. This is seen, for

instance, in the ambition to find the grave of the legendary
Forfather Czech, or pagan sacrificial areas, etc.

Jan Kollár (1797–1853), an outstanding Czech philologist, was
the first to be appointed Professor of the Slavic Antiquities at
Vienna University. Unfortunately, he did not fully understand the
meaning of archaeology and that is why his contribution to the
archaeology of the Slavs remained limited. Only Jan Erasim
Vocel (1802–71), the first Professor of Archaeology at Charles
University in Prague, can be labelled the founder of the discipline
in Bohemia. In addition to being the author of the first integrated
work on Czech prehistory he gave birth to the journal *Památky
archeologické* (*Archaeological Monuments*) which, since 1854, has
been the leading archaeological periodical in Bohemia.

Undoubtedly the greatest contribution to the establishment
and expansion of the archaeology of the Slavs was made by the
founder of this special archaeological discipline, Prof. Lubor
Niederle (1865–1944). His multi-volume work *Slovanské starožit-
nosti* (*The Antiquities of the Slavs*), published in 1902–24, became
a milestone in research into the history of the Slavs and still serves
as a rich source of, for example, the forgotten traditions of
original Slavic folk culture.

In Bohemia Slavic archaeology was institutionalised through
the establishment of the Institute for Slavic Studies (1928–30) in
which experts in archaeology, linguistics, history and ethnography of the ancient Slavs were engaged. This Institute was
renewed after World War II and altogether seven volumes of
proceedings, *The Origins and Beginnings of the Slavs*, came out. In
1963 the Institute was abolished and the members left for specialised institutes of the Czechoslovak Academy of Sciences.

Poland has an outstanding position in Slavic archaeology especially in the post-war period, and has a leading position in the
studies of the Slavs. Extensive investigations and excavations
performed by many distinguished experts (of them let me name
just J. Kostrzewski, W. Hensel and L. Leciejewicz) resulted in a
huge publication project called *Słownik Starożytnosći Słowiańskich* (*The Encyclopaedia of Antiquities of the Slavs*) which has
been issued since 1961. In addition a special journal which deals
with Slavic archaeology has been edited in Poland: *Slavia Antiqua*
serves as an international platform for experts from all the
countries in which Slavs have featured in history.

2. A pottery vessel decorated with wavy lines: for many decades this pattern has been considered a characteristic expression of the Slavic sense of ornamentation.

Research into the Slavs in the German Democratic Republic has been widely supported and systematically conducted. It is headed by J. Herrmann, the Director of the Institute of Archaeology in Berlin, who is the editor-in-chief of the collection *Die Slawen in Deutschland* (*The Slavs in Germany*). The tradition of investigating the ancient Slavs in Germany (the original early medieval Slavic settlement reached almost the Elbe estuary) was founded by a prominent German scholar, R. Virchow. It was he who, in the 1870s, identified finds of Slavic origin – pottery decorated with wavy lines – in the territory between the Elbe and Vistula. These finds came mostly from fortified sites and Virchow introduced a new designation to the ancient Slav epoch – the Hillfort period – which remained in common use until today (for instance, in the Czech chronological scheme of the early Middle Ages).

Soviet archaeology has also contributed extensively to our knowledge of the history and culture of the Slavs. From the 1930s onwards research was focused on the excavation of famous old Russian towns (Kiev, Novgorod); after the World War II, investigations also embraced field projects on rural settlement and problems of the ethnogenesis of the Slavs. Attention must also be given to the special discipline of archaeology in some of the central and south-eastern European countries such as Bulgaria, Yugoslavia, Romania and Hungary.

In 1965 the International Union of the Archaeology of the Slavs was established as a part of UISPP. At five-year intervals this body organises congresses alternately in Slavic countries (1965 – Warsaw; 1970 – Berlin; 1975 – Bratislava; 1980 – Sofia; 1985 – Kiev; in 1990 it took place in Yugoslavia).

Apart from archaeology, other disciplines share the effort to clarify problems connected with the origin and ethnogenesis of the Slavs as well as with forms of their cultural and historical development. In the first place linguistics must be mentioned. This comprises four sub-disciplines: toponymy, comparative philology, history of literature, and etymology. As regards ethnogenesis, of importance is the analysis of river and mountain place-names and the comparative study of the Slavic language and those of neighbouring ethnic groups; in other words the frequency of loan-words is the main subject in this study. Up to now linguists found the closest relationship between the Slavic and Baltic languages (i.e. Lithuanian, Latvian and others). It is supposed by many scholars that originally the so-called Baltic–Slavic language union existed. The language of the Slavs has also been influenced quite extensively by German and Iranian, and to a limited extent by Celtic, Illyrian and Thracian. At this point it should be stressed that towards the end of early medieval period, after the consolidation of newly-arrived Slavic groups in the new territories and after the first states had been created, twelve national languages emerged, subdivided into three groups (West, East and South Slavic). On the basis of the linguistic and archaeological evidence it is largely supposed by a majority of scientists that Slav ethnogenesis was the latest process of an ethnic group's division within the Indo-European family. Up to C6 AD no written document informs us about the Slavs and this is often cited as evidence for the statement mentioned above. It seems probable that the development of the Slavs was in progress for several centuries in close contact to the Balts. Their ethnogenetic process was completed only in the course of the late phase of the Migration period. Since then the unknown Slavs emerge abruptly from East Europe and it is the Byzantine Empire which is heavily threatened by their raids. The ensuing expansion was the logical conclusion (because generally typical also of other ethnic groups) of the ethnogenetic process. As being suggested above a uniform Slavic language existed for many centuries (down to C12) and even now people from single Slavic-speaking countries (who, incidentally, constitute 30 per cent of the European population) can understand one another better than, for example, those coming from the territories in which the population speaks some of the German languages.

As for other disciplines dealing with the history of the Slavs, they include history (written documents), ethnography and the history of the arts, and in natural science the most important are anthropology, palaeozoology and palaeobotany. Mutual co-operation amongst these disciplines and the combination of their results can lead us to meaningful research into the cultural, social and political evolution of the ancient Slavs and their contribution to all-European history in the Middle Ages, assuming that the right method is picked and the value of sources under consideration is viewed critically.

Let me try now to outline the history of Slavic expansion and the ensuing period of stabilisation which came after the Slavs (originally unified) settled permanently in vast territories of Central, South-Eastern and Eastern Europe.

There is a substantial problem which has been under discussion for many years. This is the so-called country of origin of the Slavs. Basically two main conceptions exist in this respect: 1. The Slavs came into existence in Central Europe and during their history other ethnic groups (the Celts, the Germans) invaded their homeland but never managed to annihilate or assimilate the Slavs. At the turn of Antiquity they emerged once again as a nationality and since then they have never escaped the historical scene of Europe. This theory takes no account of any expansion. 2. The Slavs originated in Eastern Europe and from there they moved westward. This theory supports the idea that the Slavs expanded from their country of origin. Today this is recognised by most scholars.

The term 'country of origin of the Slavs' is now considered dynamically, not statically. It is viewed as a large territory of elongated shape which changed its position as the Slavs proceeded from east to west.

The oldest theory on the country of origin of the Slavs is that created by Nestor, an old-Russian monk who, in his twelfth-century chronicle, identified the Slavs with the Illyrians. Thus, the so-called Balkan theory, which was not definitely displaced before nineteenth century, came into existence. According to this theory the Slavs are supposed to have originated southward of the Carpathians, in the territory of the Balkan peninsula. Another theory – about Asia Minor as the point of origin of the Slavs – was a modification of the previous one and hardly any would advocate it at present.

The most commonly held opinion now is that the Slavs originated in Europe, northward of the Carpathians, in the fertile territories of the Vistula, Dniester, Bug (the Vollynia-Podolí Lowland) and Dnieper basins. Up to now the most complicated problem is the identification of some of those archaeological cultures which occupied this area in the period before the Slavs appeared for the first time as a nationality. This is documented by contemporary historians of the earliest groups of Slavs (such as the Przeworsk culture in western areas and the Zarubincy and Chernjachiv cultures in eastern parts of the territory in which the process of Slavic ethnogenesis was in progress). These cultures apparently derived from the activity of different ethnic groups (the Slavs, Sarmatians, Dacians, Goths) since their material assemblages are linked and styles typical of those nationalities can easily be distinguished within them. In addition, all of these cultures ceased to exist by the end of the Roman period which means that between their extinction and the date of the coming of the Slavs there is a gap of at least one century.

From the geographical viewpoint the ethnogenetical process of the Slavs is connected with the vast territory of the forest steppes which borders on steppes in the south (northern Black Sea country occupied originally – in Antiquity – by nomadic tribes of the Scythians and Sarmatians and colonised extensively by the Greeks, Romans and Byzantines) and by forests, occupied mostly by Finno-Ugrics and Baltics, in the north.

Attempts have also been made to identify the Slavs with some of the tribes mentioned by ancient historians (Herodotus' Neurs, Budíns and Scythians the Ploughmen). But first of all there is a problem of the *Venedi* (*Veneti, Venadae*) who were mentioned by Plinius and Tacitus. In the German language, apart from the term

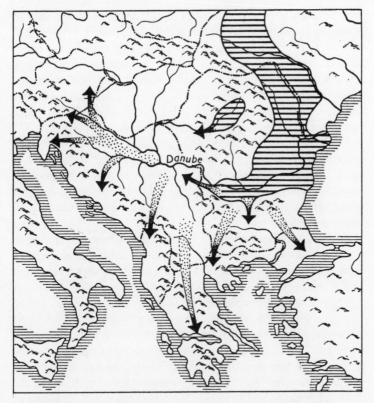

3. The movement of the Slavs to the Balkan Peninsula and Central
Danube Basin in C6–7 AD. The map is based on the combination of
various categories of historical sources (adapted after Z. Váňa 1983).

die Slawen ('the Slavs'), there existed and was in use until com-
paratively recently another expression for these people – *die
Wenden* – and, at the same time, Jordanes, one of the first historians who wrote about Slavic expansion in 6th century, specific-
ally makes the Slavs identical to the *Veneti*, so some scholars
support the idea that the Slavic groups were, during the latent
stage of their ethnogenetical process, hidden behind the latter
denomination.

The name 'Slav' appears for the first time at the beginning of
C6 AD (Pseudo-Caesarius Nazianus) but philological explication
of this name is obscure.

The Great Expansion of the Slavs begins in the first third of C6.

There are authors who point out that there are a few words of Slavic origin in vocabularies of some other ethnic groups that came to Europe before them (e.g. *proso, médos, strava* – according to Jordanes' reports these were used in the language of the Huns). It is difficult to decide whether this is evidence that the first groups of Slavs penetrated into the west as early as C4–5 AD or whether these are only loan-words adopted by the Huns before their campaign into Central and Western Europe.

There are various reasons that are taken into account when accounting for Slavic expansion. They are: an internal process of social differentiation; the effort to gain new resources; pressure by nomadic tribes (the Avars) causing exodus from the country of origin; and a simple endeavour to populate empty areas left by Germanic and other tribes.

Be that as it may, expansion resulted in a substantial change in the ethnic composition of the Continent. In this process some tribes and ethnic groups either ceased to exist or were assimilated (e.g. Thracians, Illyrians and Dacians).

The invasion of the Slavs proceeded in three directions: to the west, the south and the east. The southern expansion is the best documented in written sources. The Slavs (in Byzantine reports often named *Sklaveni*), in the course of several campaigns, passed through the territory of Moldavia along the east end of the Carpathians, and from fertile Walachia they went on to the Balkan Peninsula and to former Roman provinces in the southern part of Central Europe. Since the year of Justinian's coming to the throne (527 AD) the Slavic warriors crossed the Danubian frontier of the Byzantine Empire and towards the end of C6 they reached Greece, the Peloponnese, the Aegean Islands and even Asia Minor. This is documented particularly by place-names and, to a lesser extent, by archaeology. Occasionally they got together with some of the eastern nomads, especially with the Avars. In 626 AD the joint forces of the Slavs and Avars besieged Constantinople but failed. After this date the attacks against the Empire finished and the expansion converted into the forward march of the Slavic tribes, not only warriors, into South-East Europe. In C7 some of the Slavic groups that had colonised the south came probably also to Central Europe and brought with them some achievements preserved in the former Danubian provinces, of which a new type of pottery was the most important. The state-forming process of

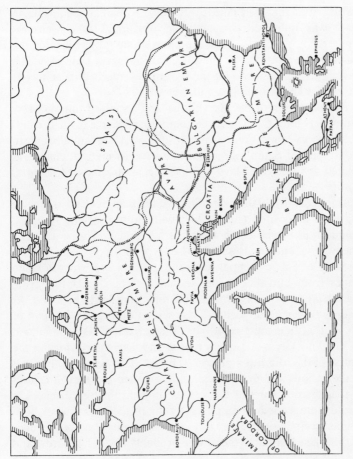

4. Europe in early C9, after the great expansion of the Slavs (adapted after Z. Váňa 1983).

Slavic tribes that permanently settled the Balkan Peninsula in C6–7 was influenced by nomadic Bulgarians who were assimilated by the Slavs. Together these ethnic groups created the Slavic–Bulgarian nation. The so-called Bulgarian Empire, which waged numerous wars with the Byzantines, reached its climax at the end of C9 and the beginning of C10.

The expansion of the Slavs to the west remained unnoticed by chroniclers until C7. The earliest important source is the Chronicle of the so-called Fredegarius. In this work we find allusion to the Empire of Samo (623–58), a pre-state formation which was created by western Slavs against the Avar raids to Central Europe.

Archaeologically the oldest Slavic settlement of Central Europe has been associated (since 1940) with pottery of the so-called Prague type which came from east Poland and west Ukraine (there it is known as the Korčak-type pottery). The earliest evidence of Slavic occupation in the territory of Czechoslovakia comes from Slovakia of the second half of C5. Dating from slightly later (the turn of C5) are the finds revealed in Moravia. As regards Bohemia, the country was settled during the first half of C6. At that time the greater part of its territory was depopulated by previous Germanic tribes that abandoned the country in the course of the Migration period. The first Slavs occupied the most fertile regions and in many cases they settled the areas and sites of their predecessors of C1–6, thus utilising their experiences in the advantageous topographical setting of habitation sites. Both linguistics and archaeology have proved a temporary coexistence of the latest Germans (these were probably the Langobards) and the first Slavs (occurrence of some place-names of German origin – Motol, Ohře, Šárka – in the country; occurrence simultaneously of typical Slavic and Germanic constructional features of houses, and pottery within one site).

In the second half of C6 the Slavs penetrated north-westward to the Central Elbe basin. There they came into direct contact with the original German population and that, together with different environmental conditions, resulted in a rather specific culture of the first Slavs in east Germany (types of buildings, pottery, etc.). At the end of C8 groups of Slavs almost reached the Elbe estuary and, at the same time, northern regions of Bavaria. Their forward march was stopped by the Empire of the Franks

5. Prague-type pottery vessel has traditionally been linked with the earliest Slavic groups in Central Europe.

and so the German–Slavic frontier remained, for three and a half centuries, on the line of the Elbe, Saale and Bohemian Forest. This boundary was patrolled by the Franks with the aid of a special system based on the existence of *marks*, special frontier territorial units organised in a military manner (e.g. *Limes Sorabicus, Ostmark*). These served as a protection against the Slavic raids and, at the same time, as starting points to the eastern military campaigns. Socio-economic development in the southern part of the western Slavic territory resulted in the establishment of the Great Moravian Empire, the first state-like formation of the western Slavs (C9) while the Polabian–Baltic tribes never managed to create a united state organisation and this caused their extinction. After the fall of the Great Moravian Empire the state-forming process accelerated in Bohemia and Poland and was crowned with the emergence of early medieval states in C10–11.

Almost nothing is known about the Slavic expansion to the east. Probably the earliest Slavic population in those territories were the Ants (*Anti*). Jordanes equated them with *Veneti*. These are reported by him to have occupied the Dniester and Dnieper basins (C4–7). They are said to have established a tribal union

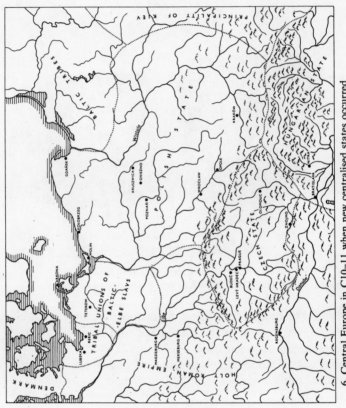

6. Central Europe in C10–11 when new centralised states occurred (adapted after Z. Váňa 1983).

which was annihilated by the Avars in 602 AD. For certain reasons (the name itself of the Ants is not Slavic, but probably Iranian in origin) it is assumed by many scholars that the Ants originally had been the Iranians but later were extensively influenced and assimilated by the Slavs. It is difficult to identify any early medieval cultures with the Ants.

West of the Dnieper the first Slavs are commonly linked with the culture of the Korčak-type pottery, with the Peňkovka type (this is often equated with the Ants) and perhaps with the Tušemlja-Koločin group (the whole area of the upper Dnieper basin); all of them are dated C6–7 and were followed by the Luka-Rajkoveckaja type in C8–9.

East of the Dnieper the culture of Romny-Borševo existed between C6 and C10. The state-forming process in eastern Slavic territory resulted in the rise of the Principality of Kiev, a powerful east-European state which strongly influenced events in that part of the continent, and cultural and commercial relations between the Vikings and Byzantine Empire as well.

Thus, after the Great Expansion the settlement process of the Slavs was crowned with the formation of early medieval states (or state-like units) of Great Moravia, the Czech and Polish states in the west-Slavic country, the Bulgarian Empire in the South and the Principality of Kiev in eastern territory.

2

The ancient Slavs' habitation sites: from simple communities to sophisticated castles and urbanised centres

In the process of searching for the social structure of the early Middle Ages (the period in which Central and Eastern Europe was populated by the Slavs) the investigation of settlement forms and the mutual relations between their single components stand to the fore in current Slavic archaeological studies. With regard to the fact that relevant written sources are small in number (this is true especially for the first stage of the early medieval period) it is clear that a decisive role in such process must be played by archaeology, although it co-operates with a number of other disciplines.

Settlement forms and material culture were spread by sixth-century expansion throughout vast territories of Europe. In this context let me mention the so-called 'Slavic cultural unity', a term introduced and used by some Czech and Polish post-war scholars. The idea is that similarities in material culture of territories newly colonised by the Slavs are considered as relics of a previous cultural unity and consequently of a unified ethnogenetical evolution. Apart from similar forms and decorative components of pottery (for example the multiple and single wavy-lines), rites (cremation), and some kinds of jewels (especially the S-shaped earrings) it is, most of all, rural residential buildings that, having been widely scattered in Eastern and Central Europe, may indicate the original cultural unity of ethnic groups that had completed their ethnogenesis and started to expand. In the course of subsequent centuries cultural unity disintegrates step-by-step because of the internal development of Slavic tribal society and influence from outside. There are, of course, local differences in

16

7. Variability in the wavy-line ornaments of the earliest medieval pottery (C6–7) from central Bohemia.

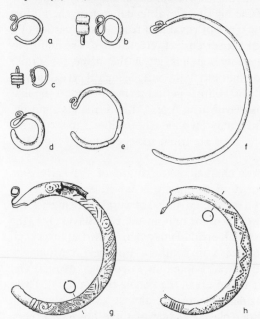

8. Lock (Ear)-rings with S-shaped terminals, a typical sort of medieval jewel considered by traditional Slavic archaeology a typical grave item produced by the ancient Slavs (after *Die Slawen in Deutschland*).

the quality and extension of this evolution. The western Slavic tribes were increasingly influenced by the power politics of the Frankish (and later East-Frankish) Empire and from the end of the first millenium they started to orientate to the Western European cultural environment. The Slavs who settled in south-east Europe come into contact with the Byzantine culture and the east Slavic tribes have vivid connections with the Vikings (Varangians).

As regards the initial period of expansion (mid-C5–6) we know about the existence of more-or-less uniform unfortified rural habitation sites. In general, since C7 a new phase of settlement activity occurred as a consequence of the transition to a sedentary way of life, the building of permanent settlements and the gradual formation of tribal–geographical units. It is the hillfort that became the typical component of ancient Slav settlement practice. The history of this form of habitation site finished only at the turn of the early medieval period, C12–13, when, in connection with the collapse of the administrative system of the early states and with the coming of the high medieval feudal system, the hillfort ceased to exist. New types of royal and feudal stone castles of a West European form were extensively erected then. The hillfort as a characteristic phenomenon has given the name (or rather archaeological denomination) to the early medieval period in west Slavic territory (i.e. the Hillfort period as mentioned in the first lecture). A comparison with Iron Age (Celtic) Britain is apposite, for the role of hillforts may then have been similar in settlement distribution as in the pre-state tribal societies of the west Slavic countries.

Probably the most characteristic feature of the early Slav culture in the majority of the newly occupied territories is, in addition to pottery, residential units of rural settlements, the remains of which we trace not only in the east Slavic area (the Ukraine: the cultures of Korčak, Peňkovka, Luka-Rajkoveckaja, Romny-Borševo) but also in southern Europe (in Moldavia: Suceava-Şipot; in Bulgaria: Popina; in Yugoslavia: Muśići) and with the west Slavs (the culture of the Prague-type pottery). These are sunken rectangular features of almost square plan with heating stone facilities placed in one of these houses' corners; occasionally remains of internal construction and equipment components have been found. We call them sunken or semi-

9. Sunken-floored building with stone oven in a corner: the most common type of rural residential structure in central and eastern Europe of the early Middle Ages.

10. Lštění: a characteristic example of early medieval Czech hillfort (in this case with a baroque church which is supposed to have had a Romanesque predecessor) situated on a promontory above the confluence of two streams. A typical landscape of the south-east hilly region of central Bohemia is visible in the background.

11. Hazmburk (north-west Bohemia, C14): an example of the west-European stone castle form expresses new ideas in building fortified units that came to central Europe in connection with the establishment of the feudal system in the C12–13.

sunken houses (huts), the sunken-floored (or featured) buildings of English and *Gruebenhäuser* of German terminology.

As the most extensive and complex excavations of early medieval habitation sites have been carried out in eastern and western areas of the Slav territory, we shall turn our attention to these areas.

Basically two regions can be distinguished within the territory. These are: 1. That in which sunken houses occur; this applies to the central section and parts of the north-east section of the area under consideration. 2. That in north-west part in which above-ground timber houses appear. Our knowledge of this type of residential building is relatively poor owing to the less favourable environmental conditions for tracing them.

In comparison to the country situated west of the Elbe (the German settlement domain), the composition of the built-up cores of rural sites in Central and East Europe is different. Here the residential units prevail absolutely and this is true for both territories mentioned above. The presence of storage pits (granaries) situated mostly in the vicinity of the sunken huts is relatively common. Although in some sites the number of various non-regular pits in sections and plans is high, the occurrence of features that could be explicitly interpreted as outbuildings is rare. The uniformity in residential units, i.e. comparative in-variability in their size, forms and inner equipment, is one of the principal arguments that this reflects a simple society based on socially unstratified family communities. The distribution of in-dividual farms spread randomly in rural settlements, which is common in German territories, is almost unknown in Central and Eastern Europe until the end of first millenium. Exceptionally, such an arrangement was revealed in the region of the Polabian Slavs where hamlets placed in the vicinity of several hillforts had fenced farm-like layouts.

In general there are three interpretations of the sunken huts: 1. They are one-room residential units; 2. They are the sunken sections of bigger above-ground buildings; 3. They are the remains of old-Slavic baths known from historical and ethno-graphical sources.

They are widely considered to be typical emergency buildings constructed in periods of transition. In this respect some scholars point to the fact that they frequently occur in the context of the

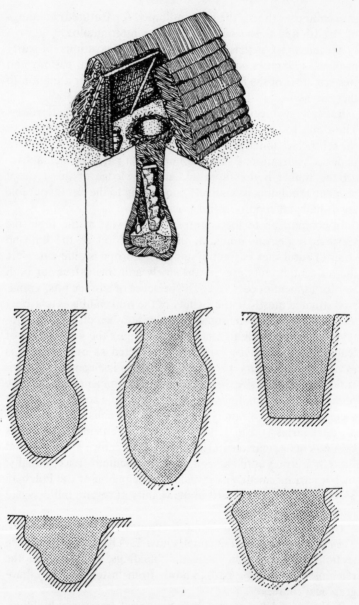

12. Types of early medieval storage pits in Bohemia: sections and a reconstruction (after J. Kudrnáč 1970).

oldest refuge sites (hillforts) characterised by plain hand-made pottery, and buried hoards of objects – namely, with components of a similar causal nexus. In my opinion it is not possible to agree absolutely with the assumption that these remained emergency buildings because sunken-floored buildings survived through several centuries, long after the final stage of the Slav expansion. It has been proved that this type of feature prevailed in regions with a continental climate of extreme temperatures within single seasons. They appear in areas with dry (loess) soils, not wet.

As regards the above-ground buildings, they were of timber (beam) construction rather than wattle and daub. They were revealed in Mecklenburg, Lusatia and lately also in Czechoslovakia (south Moravia – Mutěnice). In most cases they were of oblong ground-plan and equipped with open hearths.

Early medieval Slavic habitation sites dating from the end C5 to C7 have been extensively excavated and this enables us to characterise the forms of settlement activity of the first phase of the early medieval period. Since the mid-fifth century settlement units of different extensions appear in west Slavic territory (the present states of Czechoslovakia, Poland and the German Democratic Republic). These units are almost the same as those in Eastern Europe (the Ukraine) both in arrangement and in the similarity of features found in them. The habitation sites in west Slavic regions used to be mostly somewhat smaller in plan but the quantity of features was relatively high (in Dessau-Mosigkau, for instance, there were five hamlets in an area of 120 × 60 metres); but mostly these are the remains of several phases of just one or two settlement units which were relocated during the period of their existence. The oldest East European sites can be characterised as areas which were placed in river valleys and usually separated by distances of more than one kilometre.

It is possible to generalise that the settlements are distributed in irregular clusters and that this is a reflection of both the site relocations and of the existence of a few hamlets within one settlement phase. Single residential units are arranged either irregularly (in clusters) or into more-or-less regular rows or semi-circles and circles. In the west Slavic territory one core usually included slightly fewer residential buildings (approximately eight to ten) than in the east (more than ten) and it is assumed that some forty to fifty inhabitants lived there (one family occupied one

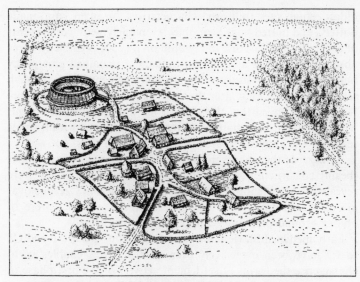

13. Reconstruction of irregularly laid-out farmsteads constituting a settlement unit supported by a fort in Tornow, lower Lusatia, Germany; C7–8 (after *Die Slawen in Deutschland*).

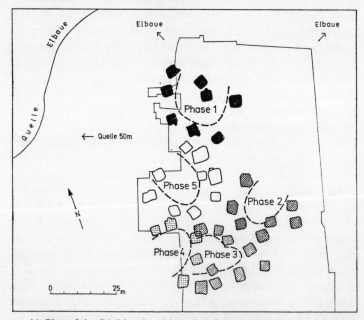

14. Plan of the C6–7 hamlet with sunken-floored huts in Dessau-Mosigkau, central Elbe basin, Germany (after B. Krüger 1967).

building). In some sites the evolution from cluster to regular arrangement has been shown. In some scholars' opinion this already represents the early phase in which the three basic types of habitation sites emerge as they are known in our environment in high medieval times. However, we should by no means perceive intentions similar to those connected with regular nucleated high medieval villages.

From the environmental point of view, the close linkage of early Slav settlements to rivers must be stressed. Mostly they were built in fertile soils situated below the 300-metre contour. Almost exclusively the traces of settlement activity have been found in regions covered originally with oak and hornbeam woodlands and riverine forests. In Bohemia, for example, the occurrence of Slavic sites in those areas occupied by their German predecessors is frequent. The settlement of the Roman and Migration periods was, in comparison to the period that followed, more extensive and in a few cases the Germans settled areas situated higher than 300 metres above sea level. If we compare this with the earliest phase of the Anglo-Saxon period in England, which comes within the same chronology as the early Slavic stage in Central Europe, we note that, whereas in Bohemia rural settlements established by their founders in the most fertile parts of the country, extensively depopulated in those times, prevail (although we have also some evidence that sites situated in strategic positions were occasionally occupied), in England the rural sites – often very large, e.g. Mucking – used to be established at rather higher altitudes which were somewhat unfavourable, and only later did they move to river valleys.

Our knowledge of rural settlement forms of the Hillfort period (C8–12 approximately), especially of its late stage (C11–12), is very fragmentary, although from the documents we have information on the existence of newly established colonisation villages of special character (the place-name types of Újezd and Lhota). In Bohemia only one hamlet dated C8–9 was extensively excavated (Březno): in the first phase the huts were arranged in a semicircle (the central-square type) while later the layout was changed so that the buildings were rearranged into rows (they lined the confluence of the river Ohře and a local brook). The spatial arrangement of a hamlet from the late stage of the Hillfort period is known from the single site of Opolánky in the east part of

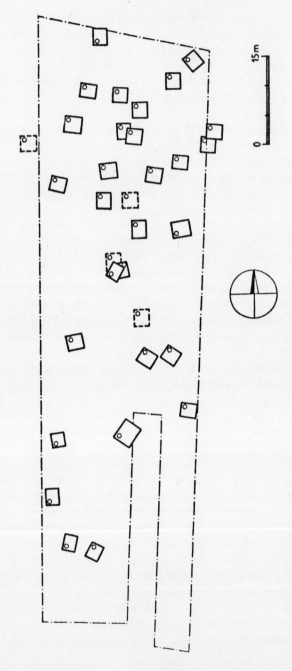

15. Seeming irregularity in domestic buildings arrangement is underlaid by similarity to the form of the building excavated: this is rather a reflection of repeated settlement activity (see the intrusive features) which may have obscured regular lay-outs of single hamlets (Roztoky, central Bohemia, C6; after Gojda-Kuna 1986).

Central Bohemia. In the second half of C10 a habitation site was constructed in the same place where settlement existed in C6–8. It was fortified and its area bisected: the western part was fenced by a huge stockade, the eastern one by a ditch with a palisade built in to the bottom. At the northern perimeter of the ditch a gate was erected which served as an entrance to the eastern part of the site. The hamlet ceased to exist at the end of the C12. Apart from the fortification, several pits, residential buildings and a pavement have been excavated there. The site can be interpreted either as evidence of a farmstead inhabited by one or more free peasant families (the so-called *allodists* who are supposed to have existed as early as C9) or as a refuge site for people from surrounding unfortified hamlets.

We know a bit more about the situation in Moravia. In the late and terminal stages of the Hillfort period (C11–13) habitation sites of moderate size prevailed: their spatial arrangement seems to be regular (Záblacany, Pfaffenschlag, Mutěnice).

The distribution of settlements in the landscape, the arrangement of features in them and their field system were fundamentally transformed in connection with the high medieval economic and social changes (i.e. the so-called agrarian revolution, external colonisation, the rise of towns and goods production, etc.).

The main source of information about residential buildings of C8–12 comes from hillforts. It is obvious that conditions in this type of settlement differed from rural milieux; nevertheless, we can obtain knowledge of building practices of that period from these hillforts since it is probable that the buildings found there used to be constructed by local craftsmen from the surrounding environment. Until mid-C9, one-room sunken huts with stone ovens prevailed absolutely. Only since that date did other forms of residential buildings appear, namely above-ground structures made of timbers or wattle and daub, often constructed as two- or three-room houses.

The fact that the Hillfort-period rural sites have been extensively detected by plough walking (e.g. in the lower Vltava basin, the region of the town of Chrudim) but almost nothing is known about their residential building appearance suggests that the buildings must have been of above-ground construction and hence were destroyed by agricultural practice. The sunken features survived, but since pottery fragments are deposited

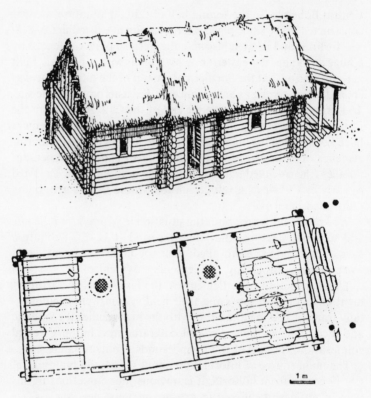

16. Ground-plan and a reconstruction of a timber house from the hillfort of Levý Hradec, central Bohemia (C9). Note the hearths in both side rooms and remains of wooden floor; the central room may have served as an entrance hall (after I. Borkovský).

predominantly in the bottom layers some 50–100 cm. down, we can detect them by fieldwalking only rarely. We can suggest that the general evolution of a residential unit started with one-room sunken-floored buildings of the early Slavic and old Hillfort periods (about the end C5 to C8). Later this type was transformed into the above-ground timber or wattle-and-daub structures in the other phases of the early Middle Ages. But it should be stressed that the sunken type of house survived until the high Middle Ages as an emergency building in the newly-established towns of C13–14.

The data about the rural house types of the turn of the first millenium in East Germany are relatively good. Excavations in settlement areas situated in the vicinity of the Mecklenburgian and Lusatian strongholds revealed evidence on the variability in size of houses in hamlets arranged into a system of farms. For example, in the Tornow old-phase, community halls (measuring up to 16 × 8 metres) situated in fenced courts have been revealed. They were surrounded by outbuildings and possibly by small gardens. In a later phase the halls disappeared to be substituted by several small houses; the number of outbuildings decreased. The proportion of structures was the highest in the best equipped courts having a network of pavements (probably attributable to the hamlet's owner).

In Moravia the country building forms of C11–12 have been uncovered recently. One-room sunken and above-ground houses prevailed there measuring generally 16–20 square metres in area. At the same time the first evidence on the existence of a two-room house (a hall as an addition to the living room) have been found. Of the outbuildings the most common are storage pits. Apart from houses and storage pits, mostly arranged in clusters, oblong sunken features were excavated in some habitation sites interpreted as chambers (granaries). Only later did these become integral parts of residential houses. Thus, the typical country house of the chamber (granary) type emerged.

When considering rural forms of settlement, the importance of the evolution of spatial arrangement should be stressed. This gives insight into the medieval landscape in which agriculture was of prime importance. In the changes of settlement cores and their field system certain developments deriving from a variety of influences can be detected. Historians and archaeologists have

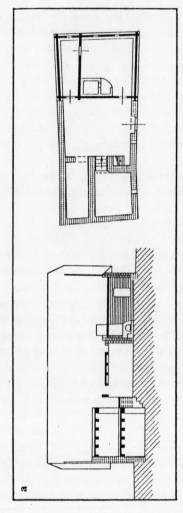

17. The chamber-type house: cross section and ground-plan (the chamber is situated on the left side and has two floors). This spatial arrangement of residential buildings comes from the late Middle Ages. The central room represents the (entrance) hall. Living room with oven is situated on the right side and is constructed of wooden timbers (after Dějiny hmotné kultury I/1).

stressed the setting of country communities in the environmental and economic context, while ethnographers have considered the ethnical features of these unit layouts. Excavations of early medieval rural sites suggest that they were adapted to environmental conditions and landscape morphology. Regular allotments have not been recognised: their introduction came only during the great changes of C13 in connection with the newly established social class of independent landlords.

Since C7 a new phenomenon of higher order – a hillfort (castle in written sources) – occurs extensively in the greater part of Slav territory. It should be noted that there are some hillforts dated even to C6 (the so-called Klenica–Tornow group) but a century passed before these settlement units were mentioned in chronicles (Fredegarius), annals and legends, and by C8 they had become quite common.

Ancient Slav hillforts then became a dominant settlement category of the Early Middle Ages throughout those Central and Eastern European territories settled after the late stage of the Migration period by the Slavs. Their occurrence south of the Danube (where formerly Roman provinces existed) was minimal since the newly arriving population used – as did the Anglo-Saxons in Britain – deserted urban centres more or less destroyed by various Germanic and nomadic tribes during the Migration period, or they founded specific vast fortified units different from typical west Slavic hillforts (e.g. Pliska and Prjeslav in Bulgaria).

In the whole west Slavic territory (the present Czechoslovakia, Poland and what was the German Democratic Republic) the number of hillforts amounted to about 3,000. Most of them were in Poland (approximately 2,000); in the basins of the Elbe and the Oder there were some 6–700 and in Bohemia about 130 (of which some 35 have been excavated more or less extensively). These settlement units were probably raised in connection with the disintegration process of the originally unified Slavic 'nation' which was in existence after the Slavs settled new territories in Europe. At that time smaller units in naturally (geographically) limited regions had been organised: castles (hillforts) become the centres of them. The first castles of C7–9 were large in plan and divided into two or three parts (the inner fortified area or acropolis, and the baileys). They can be characterised as units connected with extensive agricultural production (a number of

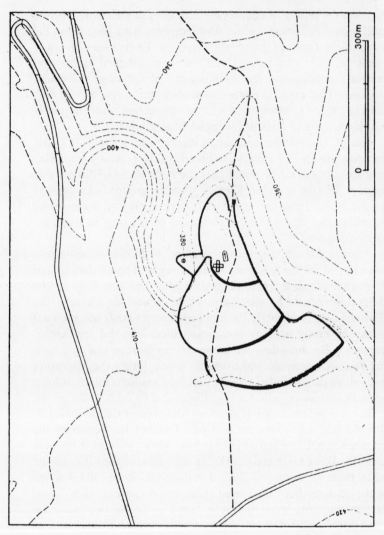

18. Libušín: an example of the typical Czech early medieval hillfort with acropolis (right on the plan) and two baileys (after M. Šolle 1984).

storage pits – granaries – were uncovered in the hillfort of Klučov in Central Bohemia; this can be compared with the Iron Age Danebury Hill in southern England which served as a local grain store. They were also utilised as refuge sites for the inhabitants of surrounding hamlets in case of danger. The finds revealed in these sites show that various types of craftsmen lived and worked there. Residential buildings prevailed in the built-up areas of these hillforts. From C9 onwards the earliest stone architecture appeared (Pre-Romanesque churches). These settlements were often built on suitably shaped hills partly fortified naturally by steep slopes, river streams or bogs. The artificially raised fortification would be constructed of material which was available in the surrounding areas. In southern parts of the west Slav territory (Bohemia, Moravia, Slovakia) the constructions comprised a front stone wall with a wood-and-earth structure, while the stone component of the fortification is absent in northern parts of west Slav regions.

Attempts at the hillfort typology based on morphological analyses of the so-called tribal territories have been criticised lately.

After the end of first millenium the size of hillforts and also their number decreased. This reflected both the gradual disintegration of tribal society, based predominantly on family relations, and the emergence of a successive process leading to the rise of early medieval states headed by princes and their great retinues. This matter will be discussed in detail in the next lecture.

In the vast territory situated between the Elbe and Oder, occupied by Elbe-Baltic Slavs, a few hundred fortified sites were erected during the early Middle Ages. Post-war excavations extensively enriched our knowledge of the ancient Slavs' way of life in that country. The most useful have been the results achieved in Mecklenburg. Four principal stages have been distinguished in the evolution of these fortifications. The oldest date from C8–9 and there are no reports on them in the written sources. They were followed by the so-called ringwalls of small size (up to 50 metres in diameter) which were associated with the emergence of noble families in the last two centuries of the first millenium AD. The third and fourth group constituted large sites internally divided into sections which occur in lake districts. They used to be constructed on islands that were connected by means of wooden

19. Round church – rotunda – on the top of the hillfort of Budeč is the oldest still-standing Preromanesque structure in Bohemia (end C9–early C10): its original dome is hidden under the roof. The tower is a C12 addition.

20. Levý Hradec, Central Bohemia, represents those fortifications which were situated on promontories and partly protected naturally by steep slopes. Compare Fig. 21.

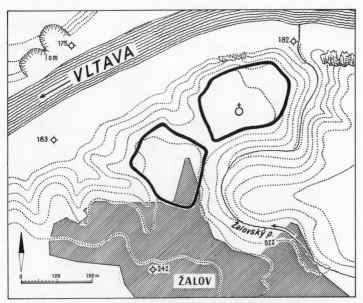

21. Plan of the bailey (left) and acropolis (right, with the church symbol) of the hillfort of Levý Hradec (after J. Sláma 1989).

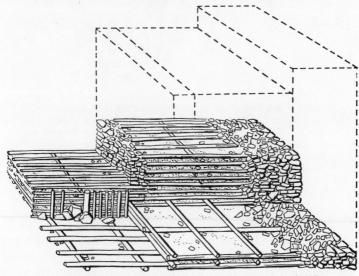

22. Stará Kouřim, central Bohemia: a typical example of the fortification consisting of front stone wall and wood-and-earth construction (after M. Šolle 1984).

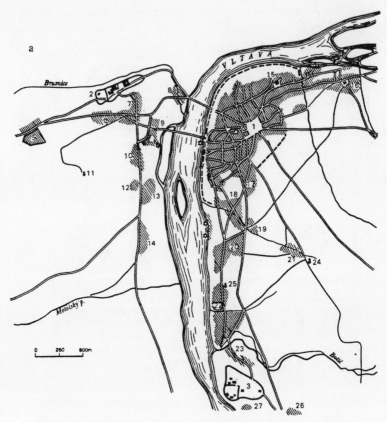

23. a) Settlement accumulation of market and craft communities (C11–13) in that part of the Vltava basin which later developed to what is now Prague: 1. area that later became the Old Town; 2. Prague Castle; 3. Vyšehrad Castle. More than forty Romanesque churches were established there. b) Prague area between 1230–1348. The most important cluster of settlements on the right bank of the Vltava (the Old Town-1) was fortified in the 1230s and the Lesser (then called the New) Town situated under the castle was founded in the 1250s and also walled, see No. 2 (after J. Čarek and V. Lorenc).

bridges and pathways with the mainland. They date from C11–12 and some of them were described by historians of those times (Ibráhím ibn Jákúb, Saxo Grammaticus). They reflect the actual necessity of defence which the tribes of Obodrits and Lutics had to organise against the German Empire. Of the best excavated sites, Teterow, Behren-Lübchin and Sukow should be mentioned.

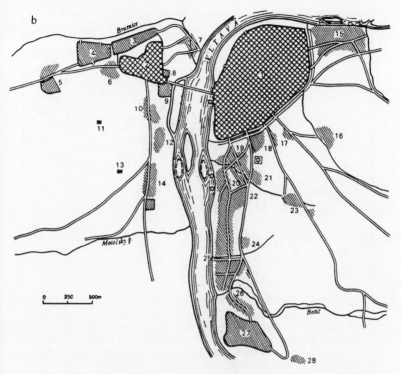

Their debris, which remained well preserved due to good soil conditions, symbolise the tragic annihilation of the north-west Slav groups at the turn of early medieval period. The Slavs who settled in that country never formed a unified organisation which would be able to defend its territory. Moreover, they never accepted the Christian faith that could have cemented their internal unity and, at the same time, would rob the enemy of the pretext for aggression. The last centre of Slavic paganism – Arkona in Rügen – was captured in 1168 by the Danish king Waldemar.

Another form of settlement activity existed, namely the urban-like (urbanised) units. Many of them developed from hillforts (the castles of written sources) – they will be referred to in detail in the next chapter – the centres of princely power which, after the turn of the first millenium AD, were enlarged by joining with the adjacent craftsman villages in their area. The so-called pre-location (pre-urban) agglomerations are typical in west Slavic

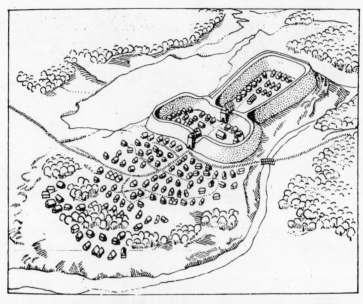

24. Gniezno, Poland: the seat of the first rulers of the Piast dynasty and of the first Polish archbishopric, is a good example of the development of those processes in which a hillfort with its adjacent settlements was transformed into the centre of political, clerical and economic life of the respective country: the whole unit is gradually urbanised: a) C8–9; b) C11 (reproduced from M. Šolle 1984).

territory and played an important role in the process of town evolution in Central Europe.

A lot of urbanised settlement units developed on the Baltic coast, some of them also inland. In many cases they became the centres of international trade as has been detected by the long-term excavations of Polish and German archaeologists. In Opole, for example, the inner area of the site was built up by timber houses arranged into streets with wooden pavements. A similar situation was revealed in the port towns of Gdańsk and Sczecin (Stettin). It has been estimated that several thousand people inhabited those sites. The most famous of them was Wolin (Vineta), or Jómsburg of some written sources, situated on an island in the Oder estuary. Chronicler Adam of Bremen suggested that Wolin was the largest European town inhabited by the Slavs. The fame of the town peaked between C9 and C11 when it was firmly fortified and equipped with a lighthouse. The excavations

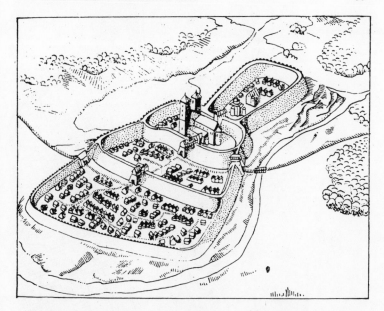

revealed evidence of highly developed crafts (pottery, wood-carving, jewel- and glass-making, etc.) and extensive commercial contacts with the East (Novgorod), Rhineland and especially Scandinavia (the Viking merchants had their emporia in that country). Wolin used to be one of the most important crossroads of commercial activity and a reloading urban centre for both western and eastern merchants. The archaeological evidence shows that settlement activity around this centre was extensive.

Some sites in the east-Slavic territory were also urban in character. The metropolis of the Russian north regions used to be Novgorod. It was bisected by the river Volchov into the seats of the profane and clerical heads of the town's republic-like form-ation. Apart from churches and palaces, remains of multi-room timber houses and workshops of Novgorod's renowned crafts-men (potters, smiths, jewellers) have been excavated. These were situated in several town wards. Archaeological investigation of Novgorod was extremely profitable in uncovering evidence of life in this centre in medieval times. Thanks to favourable soil con-ditions the features were preserved very well and so it was possible to date wooden buildings exactly by means of dendrochronology (e.g. the wooden pavement in one of the city's wards had

25. Plan of C10 Novgorod, Russia with the castle (3), cathedral of St Sophia (2) and regular street network (adapted after M. Beranová 1988).

twenty-eight phases constructed between mid-C10 and mid-C15). The street network was regularly planned and equipped with drainage. The total number of inhabitants of Novgorod may have amounted to 20,000 in C11 and 50,000 in C13 which was rare in any part of Europe.

Another large centre was the capital of the early medieval state of the Kiev Principality. In C11 the fortified core of the city (100 hectares) consisted of courtyards belonging to the prince and members of his retinue, and of clerical architectural precincts. In C12 the suburb was also fortified and craft and commerce flourished there.

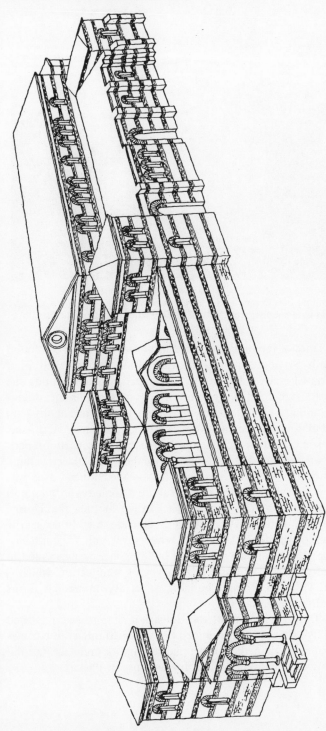

26. Reconstruction of the so-called great basilica in Pliska, Bulgaria: the building had three parts (the narthex, porticus and church itself) and is almost 100 metres long. It is suggested that it may have been the place in which the Bulgarians accepted the Christian faith (after Z. Váňa 1983).

27–28. Nin and Zadar, Dalmatia: two examples of one principle –
central lay-outs in early medieval church building. The former has a
round nave and four rectangular apses, the latter is a huge rotunda with
three eastern apses of semicircular plan.

Evidence of the process toward urbanism has also been found
in south Slavic territory. The capital of the so-called First
Bulgarian Empire – Pliska – was founded probably during the
reign of Krum and Omurtag in C9. Step by step this site, originally a military camp, was changed into a vast metropolis with
stone buildings, pavements, a water pipeline system and drainage.
It was some 23 square kilometres in area and its trapeziform perimeter was surrounded by a massive earthen wall 20 metres high.
In the centre of the fortified site the so-called Inner Castle was
constructed with an area of 0·5 square kilometres in plan and
fortified by a wall of stone blocks. Inside its area the Throne
Palace and Citadel were situated. Outside this Inner Castle
remains of the biggest church architectural unit of south-east
Europe have been excavated. The building is a basilica dated to
the end of C9. In addition to this type of architecture, which is
linked with the Roman building style, Byzantine-like forms
(central layouts) were uncovered.

In 893 AD the capital of the Bulgarian Empire was relocated
from Pliska to the newly founded Prjeslav. Although this city was
less extensive than the former metropolis its architectural and
decorative forms were as amazing as those in Pliska.

An outline of the settlement forms of the ancient Slavs tends to show that the evolution from early rural sites through to the hillforts and urbanised units was a process conditioned by a set of internal circumstances and external influences. The differences between people on the basis of their possessions and their corresponding status within an originally homogeneous tribal society increased with the increase of the economic base. The building of fortified units reflected such a process. The possibility of making a certain proportion of people free of agriculture conditioned the development of specialised crafts which, hand in hand with commerce, found its form in the building of sites with densely built-up areas of regular arrangement. This process was influenced by inspiration from the outside and this is true of political and economic, as well as artistic forms. I have aimed to show how varied and dynamic this evolution was in single territories of the old-Slavic part of Europe in the early Middle Ages.

3

Early medieval castles – hillforts – and their role in the state-forming process of Bohemia

As suggested in previous lectures a fortified site was the characteristic form of settlement activity in the early Middle Ages in almost the whole territory of the west and east Slavs. Within that vast space several regions with hillforts of specific forms and layouts occur. One of them is Bohemia. It was Czech early medieval (Slavic) archaeologists who have always had a prime interest in this sort of site; even now the strategy of this branch of archaeology in Bohemia is based on the excavation and study of fortified settlements – hillforts. This has recently been challenged by some scholars who point to the fact that the investigation of rural sites, which had direct economic relation to fortified centres, has been neglected. There are several reasons why hillforts have been excavated in preference to rural sites: 1. Many of them are mentioned in various documents, mostly in connection with the rise of a tribal aristocracy and especially with the expansion of the Přemysl (Premyslid) family that later became the ruling dynasty of the early medieval Czech state; 2. They were the political, clerical, economic and cultural centres of those times; 3. In many cases their setting in the landscape is dominant and so they understandably attract attention; 4. The excavations carried out on these sites are effective because they usually uncover a long period of settlement activity, the remains of which are relatively well preserved.

As regards terminology, the Czech denomination of this sort of site is *hradiště* (etymologically this means a deserted castle area). This was derived from the word *hrad* (castle) – *grad* or *gorod* in Old-Slavic language – which at present is used for the typical

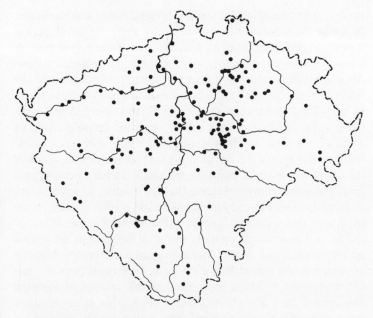

29. Early medieval hillforts in C8–11 Bohemia: map showing their quantity and spatial distribution (after J. Sláma).

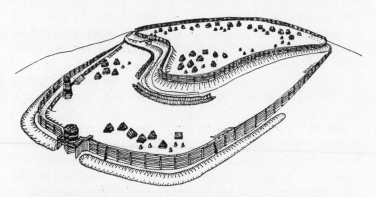

30. Klučov, central Bohemia ranks among the earliest hillforts in Bohemia. The picture shows the second building phase (C9) when the open settlement area in front of the fortified hill was enclosed with stockade and moat (after J. Kudrnáč 1970).

stone fortified buildings of medieval feudal rulers and landlords. In Latin documentary evidence of the early medieval period (legends, chronicles, annals) sites such as these are termed as follows: *civitas* (*metropolis*), *urbs*, *oppidum*, *castellum*, *castrum*. Although this terminology does not define unambiguously the relevance and size of a castle there are certain rules in using them. In the oldest documents (e.g. those of the so-called Bavarian Geographer of C9) the word *civitas* meant the fortified centre of a tribal territory which was composed not only of a castle (hillfort) but also of the surrounding area and rural sites of which the castle was a nodal point (in the social, rather than the geographical sense). This is evidence that the integrity of a centre and its hinterland was already grasped in early medieval times in the same way that we have recently 'rediscovered' it.

The evolution of Czech early medieval castles can be divided into three principal stages. Archaeologically our earliest hillforts are dated to the period between C8 (in some cases perhaps end-C7) and mid-C9. These were small simple centres of agrarian character. I have already mentioned the Klučov example: there were some sixty grain storage pits uncovered in an area of 1·6 hectares. The residential buildings were of the same type (sunken-floored buildings) as those dated to the early Slavic period, the fortification was made exclusively of wood and earth (not of stone) in the form of a rampart lined by an outer ditch. Since approximately the beginning of C9 large 'tribal' hillforts were constructed. They used to be divided into the inner area (acropolis) and one or two outer areas (baileys). Inside these centres not only were residential buildings found, but also cemeteries, cult precincts and evidence of crafts activities. Some of them have been excavated systematically in the post-war period (e.g. Budeč with an area of 23 hectares and Stará Kouřim, 44 hectares).

The third group – the latest one – represented relatively small princely and administrative hillforts. They appeared hand-in-hand with the emergence of the Přemysl princes at the end of C9. The division of hillforts into two or three parts continued but the size of their areas decreased (ranging from 5 to 10 hectares) owing to a tremendous change in its function: it became the political and administrative unit of the newly-established ruling class that resulted in new territorial organisation of the Czech country (the original 'tribal' hillforts served probably also as refuges for people

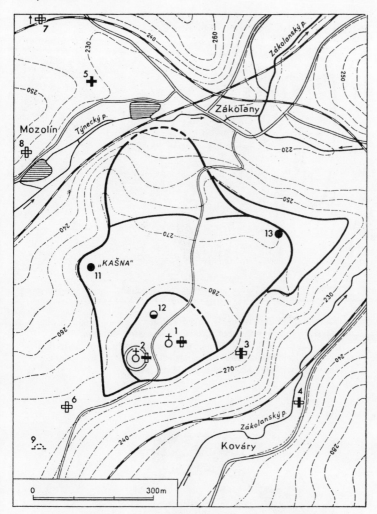

31. Plan of the early medieval hillfort of Budeč, central Bohemia with two churches and two cemeteries in the acropolis and evidence of settlement activity in the bailey and surrounding area outside the walled unit between C9 and C13 (after M. Šolle 1984).

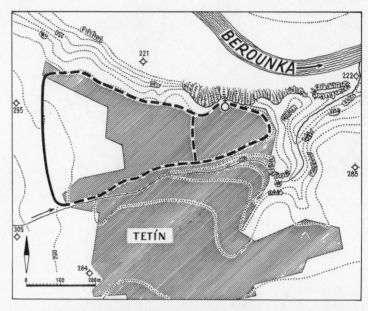

32. The Tetín hillfort is closely linked with the original domain of the Přemyslid dynasty in the south-west part of central Bohemia. It is a typical example of the C10 administrative centre with a church in that part of the castle which used to be smaller (acropolis) than the other, but central in its significance (after J. Sláma 1989).

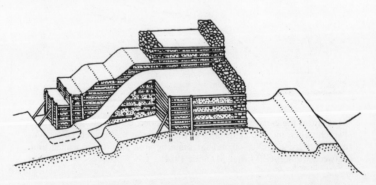

33. The 'Přemyslid wall': a reconstruction based on archaeological excavation (Bílina, north-west Bohemia, C10–12; after Z. Váňa).

living in rural settlements in the castles' vicinity in cases of external menace). Typical of these castles is the absence of craft workshops: only mintage was maintained there since rulers wanted to control the coinage. As regards the fortification form it was advanced and, for illustrative purposes, is comparable to the famous *murus gallicus* of Celtic oppidums: this was the best type of early medieval fortification in west Slav territory and is sometimes called 'the Přemysl wall'. It consisted of a front stone wall built of dry-laid white quarry arenaceous marl stones. This wall was supported by a wood-and-earth construction of chamber- or grate-like form. It was completed by a system of ditches.

From the viewpoint of morphology four groups of hillforts have been distinguished: those situated on promontories (Central and North-West Bohemia), large fortified ground blocks (East Bohemia), fortified hilltops (South Bohemia), and moor strongholds.

Before discussing the role of the hillforts in the state-forming process let us look at the evolution of fortified sites into different settlement forms in later times. Some of the hillforts ceased to exist during C11–13. This was most often the case with the earliest old-Slavic fortifications and those that were replaced by newly-established administrative centres. Such a pattern was also typical in Roman Britain (see, for example, the twin settlements of Maiden Castle and Dorchester): having been captured, the tribal centre was abandoned and a new site was founded nearby. There are also hillforts that developed into real medieval stone castles.

Probably the most important are those fortified sites that were, step by step, changed into urbanised units or towns. Today we tend to be opposed to the normative, or legal, theory of town origin which starts from the premise that sites can only be considered as actual towns if they had foundation charters or town's privileges, or the inhabitants were called burghers. Those settlements that comply with criteria characteristic of urbanised sites of the late medieval period (without having gained charters) have gradually come to be recognised as towns (see M. Biddle who names twelve criteria in this respect). First of all it was advanced craft and trade that were important in the life of a castle community. The administrative units of the Přemysl castle system gradually evolved into urbanised settlements by the inclusion of

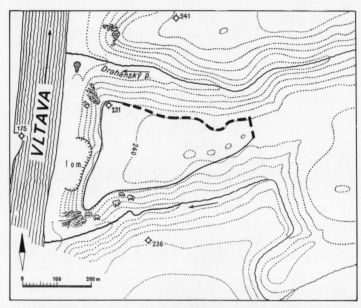

34. Bohnice-Zámka represents the hillforts situated on promontories. It is on the northern fringe of Greater Prague (after J. Sláma 1989).

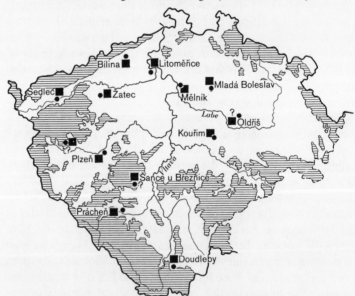

35. Map showing the distribution of twin hillforts in early medieval Bohemia. Black circles mark old 'tribal' fortified units, black squares those established as administrative centres by the Přemyslids in C10–11 (after J. Sláma 1989).

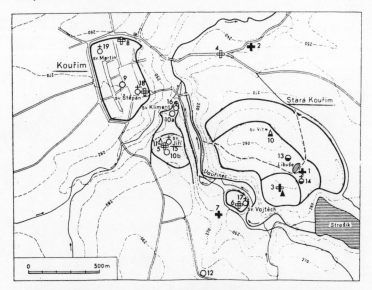

36. The Kouřim area is a good example of a regional centre that was twice relocated during the early- and beginning high Middle Ages. The original 'tribal' hillfort (Stará Kouřim) of C9–10 was displaced by the Přemyslid's administrative centre (sv. Jiří) in C11. Two centuries later it was the royal town of Kouřim that overtook the centre's role (after M. Šolle 1984).

market and craft habitation sites round them. Such development is apparent, first of all, in the case of the princely metropolis of Prague (the cluster of small communities was linked up with an important artery), of the actual district town of East Bohemia Hradec Králové, and of some other originally princely castles (Mělník, Litoměřice, Žatec, Bílina).

In the last group we can include the hillforts that had already lost their significance during the Middle Ages and the subsequent settlement activity was of a secondary order (village or hamlet). This is the case in the once-important Přemysl centre Levý Hradec (where the earliest documented Czech Christian church was founded in the last third of C9 and in which a century later the second Prague bishop St Adalbert was elected), of the centre of the Slavník family (the most powerful adversaries of the Přemysls), Libice, and some other sites. The area of Stará Kouřim can also be mentioned where three sub-sites situated close to each other provide evidence of topographical and formal changes

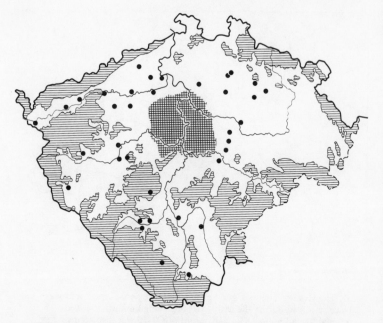

37–38. Original domain of the Přemyslid dynasty (end C9–beginning C10) in the heart of Bohemia. It was controlled by five hillforts on its borders and by three others situated in the centre (after J. Sláma 1989).

typical of a regional centre, reflecting changes in the administrative and economic sphere.

Of great importance is the study of early medieval castles in connection with the genesis of the Czech state and the organisation of its significant feature, the so-called castle administrative system. Recently performed investigations, based on existing archaeological data on the chronology and spatial arrangements of hillforts and on analysis of contemporary documentary sources concluded that within the Přemysls' territory of Central Bohemia a specific development of the castle administrative system was in progress. A synthesis of all available resources relating to the problem of the early medieval castles' role in the state-forming process in Bohemia have recently been published by J. Sláma. It is worth looking at his conclusions.

The original domain of the Přemysl family extended into the territory of central Bohemia. In that country princes of the family exercised total territorial sovereignty. Such a form of hegemony

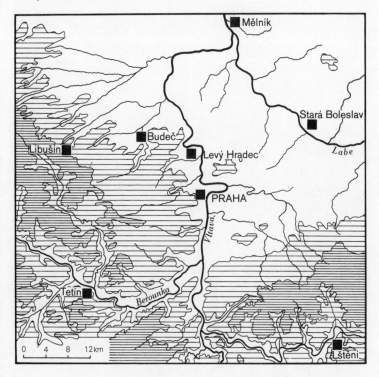

is evidenced in the extinction of old tribal hillforts and the building of new administrative units as cited in contemporary narrative documents. Some of the Czech tribes were, in the initial stage of the Přemysls' expansion, dependent on them in the form of paying tributes (*tributum pacis* in Latin terminology). Such a form is archaeologically unrecognisable. In the original domain of the Přemysl family there are nine hillforts dated to C10 that are similar in certain features. Typically churches were established there (in written sources it is noted that these buildings existed in all Přemysl castles): initially they were the private chapels of princes, later also of the members of the princely retinue who performed administrative functions; a few centuries later some of them became parish churches (C13–14).

Another feature common to these sites is their setting in the landscape. They are situated radially at more or less the same

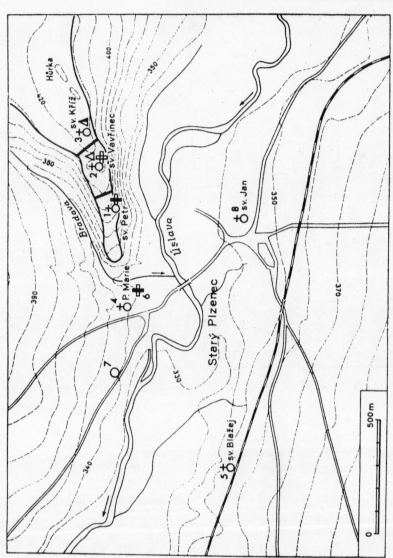

39. In Starý Plzenec, west Bohemia, churches were established in each of the three parts of this hillfort in second half C10 to C11. No. 1 (sv. Petr) is the still-standing rotunda dedicated to St Peter. Distribution of churches (Nos 4, 5, 8) suggests the existence of a densely populated agglom-

distance from Prague in buffer zones dividing the central Czech settled territory from other regions. Mostly they were built close to rivers and, in addition, on their opposite banks if looking from the direction of Prague, close to important roads. The regularity in distribution and the topographical coincidence of these sites can be considered as evidence of the objectives of their founders. Generally speaking these castles differ from the earlier hillforts. Among the new princely fortified centres it is Prague that is cited in documents most frequently. This castle is also the only one which was called *civitas metropolis*. The others used to be the seats of the members of the prince's family (demesne castles).

Thus, it seems probable that at the turn of C9 and beginning of C10 there emerged a formation in Central Bohemia which has no equivalent in other parts of the country. Prague, the centre of political power of the Přemysls, surrounded by a dense settlement network and an important market place, became the capital of the newly built state. The earliest hillforts in the Prague Hollow no longer existed, suggesting a change in the structure of administrative and power organisation which cannot be labelled a state, rather its evolutionary pre-stage.

The second phase in the development of the Přemysls' castles began when a real state of central European type started to be formed in about mid-C10 by Boleslav I. The significance of those hillforts which in C9 and the first half of C10 had been situated at the periphery of Central Bohemia as frontier defensive fortifications rapidly diminished (apart from one, none of them became a centre of an administrative district), and new castles were founded.

The results obtained by field-walking surveys and excavations are of importance. They give us evidence on the changing pattern of subordination of local tribes, originally merely tributary, to absolute dependency. The extinction of many old tribal hillforts situated outside the original Přemysl domain has been proved by archaeology. The newly organised regional centres of princely administration are often located next to the original (tribal) ones. The latter disappeared when the former appeared, so the new territorial system derived from the original one. A similar encroachment upon the original settlement network is known, for example, from Moravia in the period when it was affiliated to the Czech Principality and from the territory of the Elbe-Baltic Slavs.

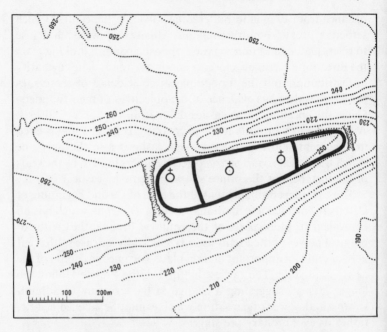

40. Prague Castle in C10 with the central inner area (acropolis) and two baileys west and east of it. Since this early period Prague has become the seat of Czech rulers (after J. Sláma 1989).

This phenomenon is one criterion considered to be characteristic of a medieval state. All of these criteria are documented by archaeological and written sources relating to Bohemia in C10–11. They are as follows: 1. The so-called castle territorial system as an expression of deliberately organised administration of the territory possessed and governed by the Prince; 2. The loss of power of old tribal institutions (extinction of the old hillforts and the building of new castles, the disarmament of the followers of tribal chiefs); 3. The reception and enforcement of Christianity as a unifying state ideology (in 973 AD the bisphoric was established in Prague); 4. The so-called duty-bound village organisation (the foundation of villages in which specialised craftsmen producing for the ruler and his grand-scale retinue's needs lived and worked; place-names in particular provide evidence of this sort of settlement); 5. The country's statutory labour (public works performed

by common people: the building and repair of castles and roads);
6. The collection of taxes; 7. The issue of coinage as a princely
right; 8. The forced relocation of the population conditioned by
economic and political reasons (the effort of the ruling class to
break off the original linkage among the members of tribal clans
and families). Thus the so-called relocated and captive villages
originated, and even today they are distinguishable by their
names. The regions and their population were named after
administrative castles; 9. New organisation of the Czech Principality's defence (building frontier military castles and fortifications).

These comments on the role of early medieval Czech castles
show the importance of a multi-disciplinary approach that takes
all resources available for the historical interpretation of medieval
reality into account. It has been shown that although each discipline dealing with the Middle Ages has its own methods and,
functions independently in analysing the respective resources
which contribute to the synthesis, it is necessary to combine the
results of all the disciplines when trying to make historical interpretations. That is the only way to attain the most objective
understanding of our history.

4

The evolution of Czech and Moravian village spatial arrangement: the socio-economic explanation

The development of the spatial arrangement of rural sites is to the fore among those medievalists who deal with the problems of country settlement. In the changes in the layouts of habitation units and their economic hinterland certain tendencies deriving from several causes can be seen. Historians and archaeologists tend to see rural habitation sites in the context of the environmental conditions and economic and social developments, while ethnographers have stressed the decisive role of ethnic factors in certain types of community arrangements. If we try to evaluate the present state of research into this problem in our country (apart from Slovakia) it is possible to say that most evidence has been gained by excavations in Moravia (the sites of the Hillfort period and some completely excavated medieval villages; an intensive surface survey in several areas together with certain special methodologies). In Bohemia, on the other hand, outstanding results on the shifts of settlement units during the Middle Ages have been achieved by means of the so-called mosaic strategy (in addition, a few deserted villages have been partly excavated); in the methodology of the surface survey very good results came from geodetic–topographic surveys of some of the deserted villages.

Since the end of C5 in the west Slavic territory of Central Europe rural sites appear of variable extension, but strikingly similar to the earliest east Slavic (mostly Ukrainian) rural communities both in terms of the resemblance and spatial arrangement of residential units in them, and in terms of the material culture. From west Slavic country we know mostly about the

58

existence of relatively small communities comprising on average between five and twenty residential units, while the earliest east Slavic habitation sites often cover extensive settlement areas (such as in Korčak). Owing to the fact that an extensive settlement area similar to those we know from the Ukraine has recently been found in Roztoky near Prague and settlement core shift has been evidenced there, we doubtless cannot eliminate the possibility that corresponding situations are hidden in some other sites, in which only one or two phases have been found, of much more extensive settlement activity (these were mostly identified by rescue excavations).

The results of the excavations carried out up to now show that individual sites tend to create variably-sized clusters, owing partly to successive replacements of individual sites and partly to the coexistence of a few contemporary hamlets in a settlement area. The residential units were organised either randomly or more or less regularly (in rows or with semicircular or circular layouts) interspersed at varying distances from one another. In the west Slavic territory a smaller number of them within one unit (approximately eight to ten) is usual; in the east Slavic region there are generally more than ten. It has been assumed that these units were inhabited by forty to fifty people in total and that one house would have been the home of one family. In some of the east Slavic settlements the evolution from random to regular arrangement has been detected.

Some twenty years ago ethnographers stated that, in the early Slavic phase of the early Middle Ages, random sites prevailed absolutely; since then archaeological excavations have proved that the most frequent spatial arrangement used to be that which we could term (morphologically) the central-square arrangement (Březno, Roztoky, Pohansko) and row (or even street) layouts (Roztoky, Pohansko, Ostrovská Nová Ves). Archaeologists in Moravia say that until the C13 the appearance of the country settlement units did not differ significantly from those described above; it is the church and manor that occur as new phenomena from the C12.

The first of the two most extensively excavated sites of the early Slavic period in Bohemia is Březno. Two complete early medieval habitation sites of C5–7 have been investigated. The earliest community consisted of twenty-one sunken-floored buildings and

41–42. In Březno, north-west Bohemia, a group of residential buildings dated to the early Middle Ages which had been excavated was experimentally re-erected. A typical 'Slavic' sunken-floored house can be seen (by courtesy of I. Pleinerová).

two to four above-ground post-constructed houses. Groups of sunken-floored features situated to the west were arranged in the shape of a circle some 50 metres in diameter, the distances between the huts varying between 16 and 27 metres. The easternmost situated group plan suggests that the huts were arranged in rows. This settlement unit is dated between the end of C5 and mid-C6 (the chronology is based on the material culture and the structural elements of the features) and has been attributed to the latest Germanic groups in Bohemia.

The other (later) habitation site in Březno occurred in two phases. The first settlement was arranged in a regular semicircle having one central structure situated approximately in the centre of the village; the extension of this community amounted to one hectare. Single huts were linked with adjacent storage pits (granaries). The number of huts in the first phase was seven to ten and these were dated to the second half of C6, the later phase to C7. Within the Březno area mutual contacts between the Slavic and German ethnic groups have been proved in the opinion of the author of the excavation project, I. Pleinerová (co-occurrence of

the constructional techniques typical of both Germans and Slavs have been uncovered; mixed material culture found in the primary refuse on the hut floors, etc.). The other extensively excavated Czech rural site of the early Slavic period will be referred to in Chapter 5 (Roztoky).

The reconstruction of field systems and the catchment areas of these early sites is a considerable problem. I. Pleinerová assumes that the landscape unit of 180 hectares can be considered the total economic hinterland of the Březno area; the central area of some 50 hectares was probably the most fertile part of the hinterland. The author devoted considerable effort to reconstructing the economic system, especially agriculture. By means of palaeo-botanical analysis the intentional alteration of seed has been proved; owing to this fact and to another one, namely the re-location of the community within the area, the practice of allowing extensive long-term fallow periods has been suggested for the Březno settlement area. As far as domestic animals are concerned, cattle were the most common but there is no evidence of stables.

The overall situation in the early Slav period has recently been outlined by M. Beranová as follows, based on the analysis of storage pits, i.e. on the ratio between their cubic capacity and their number, revealed in altogether three sites: it was relatively low population density since the ploughed fields could rotate. If we know that the people used to practice both farming and pastoralism, the plots under ploughed cultivation could be even less spacious, but relatively extensive parts of the landscape were used as pastures (including forests). In the early Slavic period the population density and the suggested farming–pastoral way of life hitherto evidenced are proportionate to each other. The cultivation was not that of slash-and-burnt practice but arable (generally the early Slavs used a wooden plough without any iron elements; the metal plough occurred just occasionally). We can assume that the so-called extensive grass-field system prevailed in agricultural production. The soils used to be sown and ploughed until the crops were relatively high and then they were converted into meadows and pastures. Experiments have shown that the cultivation of such secondary anthropogenous steps must have been within the grasp of farmers at the time in cases where an appropriate type of plough was used and the soil was furrowed to only a shallow depth. Such a method of agricultural production is very profitable and multiplication of the seed quantity is high, but there is a basic precondition of such practice, namely, relatively low population density.

As regards the setting of the early Slavic rural sites into the landscape, they were linked to streams (mostly close to the Elbe, lower Vltava and lower Ohře, but they also quite often appear close to the upper basins of brooks). Mostly they are situated in fertile soils (although sometimes we can find them at higher altitudes, mostly in places later converted into fortified settlement units – the hillforts). Traces of settlement activity are found almost exclusively in those areas where oak and hornbeam forests and riverine forests may have occurred.

As I mentioned in the second chapter, we have evidence of the co-occurrence of late Germanic and early Slavic settlements not only within a village-estate (*cadastre*) but also on the same site. The density of settlement of the late Roman period was higher in comparison to that in subsequent times, partly because later settlers penetrated into higher altitudes of more than 300 metres above sea level (the reverse is the case in the basin of the lower Vltava as found recently).

It is possible to conclude that the facts discovered hitherto about the forms of early Slavic site arrangements suggest that the

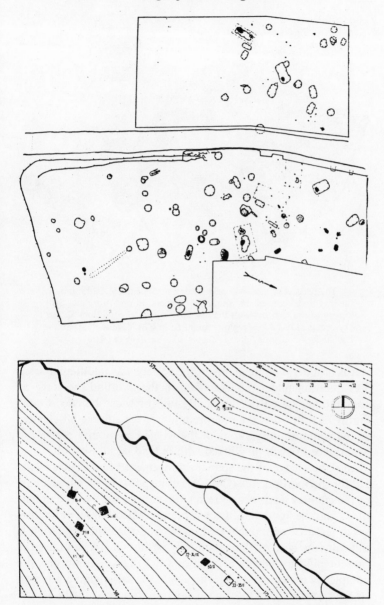

43. Dispersed plan of the site of Záblacany and regular one of the early hamlet in Pfaffenschlag. Both come from C10–13. Moravia (after R. Snášil, and V. Nekuda 1975).

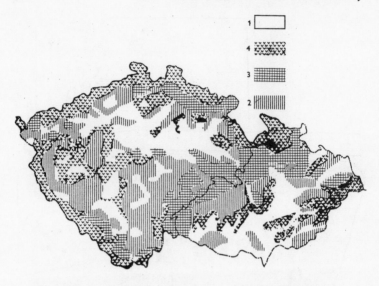

44. The process of medieval colonisation in Bohemia and Moravia: 1. the traditional core of the country's settlement in prehistory and early history as the territory with the best environmental conditions; 2. territory occupied in C13; 3. regions colonised in C14; 4. mountains and highlands–woodlands (after J. Žemlička).

status of individual members of the society was undifferentiated. The question under discussion is whether we find the stage of communities based on the family unit or those based on non-family relations (i.e. the interpretation of the storage pit clusters as the common possessions of the whole community *contra* the occurrence of such pits linked with individual households).

Our knowledge of the spatial arrangement of rural sites in the Hillfort period Bohemia (C8–12) is quite poor. In the eastern part of the country a site near Vřesník dated between the second half of C7 and the first half of C8 has been revealed but no more than seven features were uncovered; moreover, their interpretation is difficult (the core of the community is thought to be under the present built-up village area). For C8–9 there is only one site completely excavated, in Březno again: the early community had its huts positioned in the central-square arrangement with a pit in the central unbuilt-up precinct (a well?); the later community seems to have been arranged in the row pattern (the structures were situated alongside the river and tributary stream).

Of the late Hillfort period (between the second half of C10 and C12) one research and a few rescue excavations gave us a glimpse into the spatial distribution of settlements. In Opolánky-Staré Badry, a fortified hamlet of C10–12, which had its pre-fortified phases between C6 and C8, has been partly dug (this site was discussed in detail in the second lecture).

The situation in Moravia seems to be a bit better: three extensive projects have been carried out on the sites of Záblacany, Pfaffenschlag and Mstěnice. In Záblacany evidence of community replacement between mid-C10 and C13 was found. Each of the habitation sites occupied an area of approximately 2 hectares. Considering the arrangement of the domestic and outbuildings the ground-plan of the site can be characterised as a dispersed pattern with clusters of single farmsteads. In Pfaffenschlag both residential structures and outbuildings were positioned according to the row arrangement for a distance of some 150 metres. The distance between individual houses was approximately 15 metres. In Mstěnice a typical example of the central-square type was revealed. Even here the excavations revealed that the nucleus of the hamlet had been shifted, because there existed two agglomerations: 1. a cluster consisting of fifteen houses arranged into a horseshoe shape; 2. a group consisting of six buildings arranged in a semicircle. Generally we can say that the excavations in Moravia show the existence of relatively small habitation sites which tended to have a regular, rather than a dispersed arrangement.

The settlement process during the high Middle Ages (C13–15) was widely influenced by environmental conditions. In Bohemia we can distinguish two principal phases of such a process: 1. so-called internal colonisation (till C12); 2. mixed internal and external colonisation (from C13 onwards). These colonisation periods had to challenge, from an environmental viewpoint, three territorial zones: 1. The oldest settled territory was the core of settlement activity until the end of C12. It is spread below the 300-metre contour in central, east and north-west Bohemia mostly in fertile river basins with an average temperature of 8°C; 2. From the turn of C12 the remaining regions of Bohemia lying at altitudes between 300 and 500 metres above sea level (apart from the mountainous territories of the Czech–Moravian Highland and the huge ring of hilly border-ranges shaping a

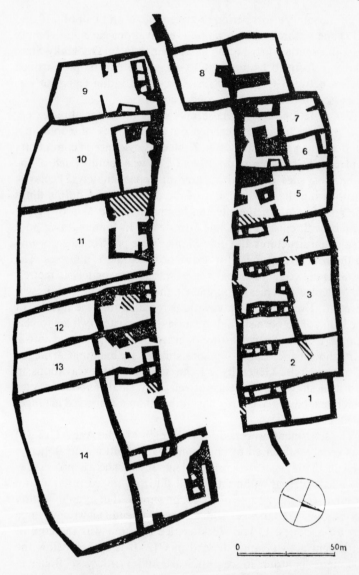

45. Deserted village of Svídna, central Bohemia. An example of the high medieval normative village with its green in the middle (after Z. Smetánka 1988).

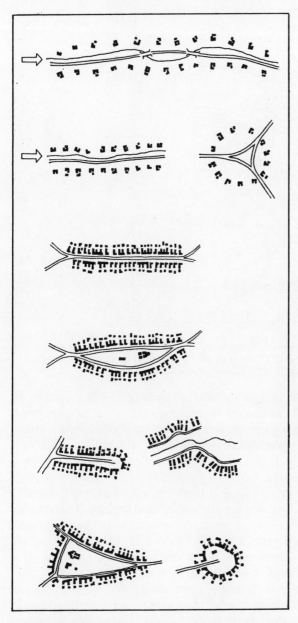

46. Morphology of Czech and Moravian medieval villages (after E. Černý).

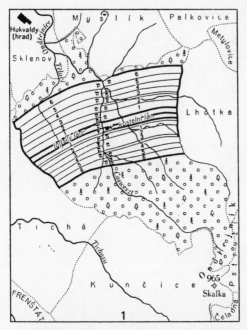

47. The so-called forest village with long narrow stripes of field units extending from the village backyards: the case of Kozlovice, north Moravia, end C13. The black symbol in the left upper corner marks a local castle plan (after Dějiny hmotné kultury I/1).

natural protection of the whole Czech territory) started to be systematically settled by domestic people at the first (internal) stage and mostly by migrants from Germany in the second phase; 3. From C14 marginal land, highlands and deeply forested territories lying at high altitude (above 500 metres above sea level) started to be colonised.

The main driving force behind this colonisation is thought to have been population growth and demand for land. The so-called agrarian revolution (or better, the revolutionary changes in agricultural practice) in Central Europe of C12–13 caused changes in landscape patterns and in the spatial arrangement of rural sites. Villages came to exist from then on with regular ground-plans and regular field systems. Towards the end of C13 random clusters of dwellings situated close to churches, and linked mostly with a lord's seat, disappeared. Instead of them we find villages with strict patterns of farmsteads corresponding to the needs of the new economic and productive technological system of agriculture.

It was the late phase of internal colonisation and the period of external colonisation which, step by step, changed the landscape and settlement structure.

The old types of villages (C12) were situated close to a water source with good access to springs or water courses, but protection against floods was also an important environmental element taken into account by the villagers. The villages mostly occur alongside streams or on natural terraces. In C13 they were often situated at the confluences of two or more streams or around springs.

As regards the ground-plans of villages we distinguish two principal formal types and several sub-types:

1. *The natural type*: 1.1, the dispersed sub-type (clusters of settled places isolated each from the other); 1.2, the compact sub-type (oval-shaped or irregular ground-plans connected with a private church); 1.3, the compact divided sub-type (two settled sites situated very close each to the other).

2. *The normative type*: 2.1, the row sub-type; 2.2, the village-green sub-type. This group reflects the organisational and probably also the administrative intentions of the settlers. These newly established villages appear as the inevitable consequence of the economic and technological changes in agriculture (the intensive three-stage rotation fallow agriculture, more extensive manuring, heavy metal plough and harrow and the introduction of harness and horseshoes).

Morphologically the 2.2 sub-type can be divided into two groups: those with circular and those with rectangular plans. The 2.1 sub-type includes the so-called road villages (those with a 'ribbon' layout along a stream or main road) and street villages (those with streets perpendicular to the main road).

In the late colonisation period (C13–15) when settlement spread out to highlands and non-fertile parts of lowlands a characteristic type of village occurred known as a forest village with long narrow strips of field units extending from the village backyards. They created very long rows of houses and their field units, some 100 metres wide and usually more than ten times that in length, have been linked with the backyards and followed up the valley slopes. Generally the central road of such a village lined

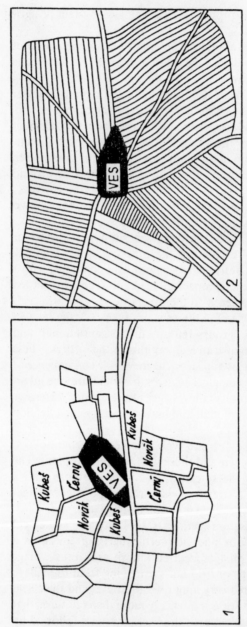

48. Types of high medieval field systems in Bohemia and Moravia (ves means village). The section system mentioned in the text is depicted in Fig. 1, the tract one in Fig. 2. Figures. 3–4 show the belt- and wedge-shaped field systems which are typical of the late medieval colonisation of highlands (after E. Černý).

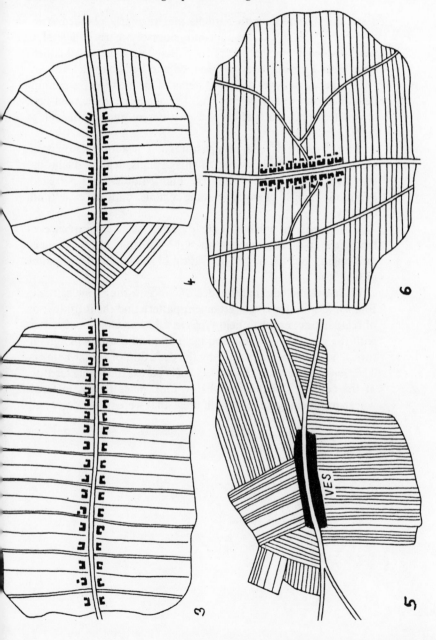

a stream. The plots with gardens and regularly planned strip-fields were linked with the threshing floor of a barn. Single plots were divided from the others by paths. Two types of this field system are known, the wedge-shaped and belt-shaped.

Of other basic types of field systems let me mention the section-field one (each section corresponds to one plot) and the tract-field system (each peasant had his plots in different tracts of the village fields).

Apart from fields, common pastures and meadows also existed. Generally speaking the system of village plans, fields and land-use that had been created during the high Middle Ages persisted, being just slightly changed in some regions, until the nineteenth century.

Most medieval villages were deserted as a consequence of landscape pattern changes in C13–14 and also of social movements and the new organisation of the landlords' economy in C15–16.

We may conclude that the idea of concentrating (nucleating in English terminology) the settlement pattern and the introduction of regular tract and belt field types in C13 had close connections with the general economic and technological changes in agriculture. They were accompanied by the desertion of earlier hamlets. The trend was not in progress regularly across the whole territory of the country. Changes probably took place fastest in fertile wheat-producing regions and in areas that were newly colonised.

5

Roztoky – The investigation of the most extensive west Slavic settlement accumulation (C6–7)

I

In connection with the present orientation of archaeology towards the study of settlement structures and relations within particular ecosystems on the level of settlement areas and micro-regions, complex explorations and investigations of geographically limited areas settled in prehistoric and early historic times are being carried out. Interactions of various scientific disciplines allow us to find answers to fundamental questions about the spatial situation of settlement units and their economic hinterland and of the relations between human communities and their environments in specific circumstances.

A contribution to this complex of problems for the early medieval period has been made by excavations at the Early Slavic settlement area on the northern fringe of the Prague Hollow on the territory of the township of Roztoky. The investigation carried out there started in 1980 as a rescue excavation owing to the reconstruction and electrification of a railway line crossing the site. Since 1987 a research project has been established aimed at the widest aspects of the early medieval settlement: the situation is favourable in that the area had largely not been occupied during the pre-early medieval times: only the northernmost part of the area was densely occupied at that times. The sequence of virtually all prehistoric cultures in the territory of Central Bohemia, from the neolithic down to the Roman period, has been detected.

It is reasonable to adumbrate the main objectives towards which the excavations have been focused. Following the detailed stratigraphy which must be of interest for each archaeologist performing the investigation of a habitation site, we try to see the settlement activity of the first Slavs in this area in connection with other evidence on landscape-use and the colonisation of the Prague region in the course of the Early Middle Ages. We try to evaluate the settlement topography and its relation to the basic components of the surrounding environment. We focus our attention on the reconstruction of the habitat and the range of intentionally produced plants and domestic animals. Owing to the fact that the site is situated immediately adjacent to the Prague Hollow and fits into the relatively dense settlement pattern of that region, and considering that evidence on early Slav occupation comes from various types of setting in the landscape (valley floors, uplands, etc.), we cannot avoid questions on the origins of the Slavic settlement and its relation to the previous German inhabitants in what is now Prague. Thus, we tend to be involved in the regional analysis of the territorial unit to which the site of Roztoky belongs.

Of the community level we try to reveal the general and specific tendencies in spatial arrangement of the early medieval habitation sites, or better their cores which, according to the evidence both from this and other excavations, comprised units of between four and ten huts, representing a single building phase which existed during the life of one generation or so. So far we are almost unable to estimate the number of similar cores making up, together with their hinterlands, a social unit or habitation site at any moment. Questions on how the spatial distribution of structures and features may help in deducing economic practice interrelated social factors are being tested.

Of importance is the contribution of the excavations to the study of one of the most frequent types of typical medieval features, the sunken dwellings. The evidence from various European territories is very rich now and attempts at the reconstruction, mostly functional, have been made. For instance, the residential character of these features in Roztoky is beyond question; the problem of whether they used to be integral parts of more extensive above-ground structures is unresolved, though some evidence on such a possibility was found during the excavations of 1987–8. The unfavourable conditions of the site for conservation of shallow or above-ground features have been

49. The site of Roztoky seen from the opposite bank of the Vltava, namely from the top of the Bohnice-Zámka hillfort. The most extensive accumulation of settlement cores was excavated in the south part of the territory (the deforested area under the steep slope on the left side of the picture).

50. The promontory of Bohnice-Zámka must have been, in C6–7, an important element of the settlement structure of the whole area investigated. Later (C8) this open site was fortified and became one of the earliest hillforts in the territory of Greater Prague.

caused by intensive ploughing and other agricultural practice in the area.

Even more important are the questions concerning the ethno-archaeological explanation of what we find today. Many problems dealing with the interpretation of such findings, like the fact that people left their houses, leaving their possessions in them and perhaps conserving them by intentionally filling the huts, leaving the sophisticated stone ovens *in situ* and not dismantling them for the purpose of gaining building material for the construction of ovens in their new houses, or questions of the male and female parts of individual houses, can be mentioned in this connection. These are problems associated with so-called post-depositional processes – primary and secondary refuse, traces of destructive processes, etc.

All the questions mentioned above are being researched in co-operation with specialists. Apart from archaeological methods and geophysics, it is the pedology and geology of the area which interests us. Some of the finds were spectrographically analysed and these analyses brought interesting results. A sample of various pottery types was submitted for special examination at the Prague University of Chemistry in order to find its firing temperature, technology, the composition of the material, etc. The results of such analyses may help to find clues to questions like whether each household unit was producing pottery vessels for its private use or whether it was being made by a specialist, and so on.

Of great importance in our approach to the investigation of the site is the analyses of ecofacts. The sources for this study are collected by flotation and screening of the fillings of the house floor-parts, and of the contents of preserved pottery vessels. Analyses of plant microremains and carbonised wood and cereal grains are carried out by a palaeobotanist involved in the project. Pollen analyses have also been performed, but unfortunately the soil conditions in the locality are unfavourable for pollen conservation. The investigation of animal bones is in progress at present. Samples for C–14 dating and geomagnetical dating were submitted to the laboratories concerned.

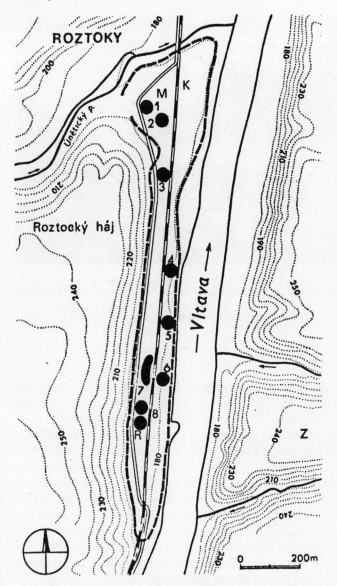

51. The clusters of early medieval rural settlements in Roztoky and the
geomorphology of the site. The promontory of Bohnice-Zámka is
bottom right, marked Z. The river Vltava leaves Prague two kilometres
south of Roztoky (after M. Gojda – M. Kuna 1986).

52–53. Two types of field archaeology on one site (Roztoky): stripping of arable layer as the first stage of research excavation by a special excavator used normally as slope-finishing machine (Fig. 52), and doing rescue activity in an artificial ditch for a gas pipe-line (Fig. 53).

II

From the geographical and morphological point of view the site is situated in a naturally limited area some 1·5 kilometres long and approximately 1–200 metres wide enclosed in a narrow valley on the left side of the Vltava river. Large-scale excavations have been carried out at the northern (6,000 square metres) and southern (4,000 square metres) ends of the area and both sub-sites were joined by three cable and pipeline trenches so that overall information pertaining to the settlement distribution within the area has become available. Since 1987 other sub-sites have been sampled through stripping of upper soil layer and excavation. All the excavated areas have yielded evidence on early Slavic settlement. The character of excavations, however, was very varied so this evidence must be evaluated accordingly.

The settlement activity is dated to the Early Slavic period, the so-called Prague-type pottery culture of C6–7 AD.

Evaluation of the character of building layout on individual sub-sites is based on horizontal-stratigraphy considerations and

on observations of details in construction and the archaeological context of individual features. Exact reference points which would permit definition of the relative ages of habitation features, however, still await identification. Preliminary departure points may be defined by components of the interior furnishings and slight differences in mobile items of the culture. In principle, the most frequent disposition of the residential building seems to have been the so-called central-square type with different variants: 1. a semicircle of 10 metres diameter composed of four or five huts spaced at regular intervals of some 6–7 metres; 2. larger semicircles of three or four huts spaced some 8–12 metres from one another; 3. a circle enclosed by seven huts, a section of which measures 30 metres. All these variants result from observations pointing to certain preliminary conclusions which will be borne out or rejected by overall analysis. Moreover, they may be distorted by the choice of the sampled sub-site within the settlement area (which we could not control up to 1986) so that what appears to be a seemingly complete ground plan of a settlement core might, in reality, have been left behind by more phases of settlement or may even continue in the unexcavated ground.

Certain indications of a linear arrangement of the rural community have been observed at only one sub-site. The total number of huts belonging to this cluster, however, is not clear (between six

54. Section of a sunken-floored building found in a pipe-line ditch. Bottom part of a pottery vessel which remained preserved on the floor of the house (left, above the number of the feature); also visible is a posthole placed just above the right side of the metre rod.

55. Another feature rescued in the artificial ditch: an earthen oven paved with stones and ceramic fragments. This may have been used for drying wheat grains.

56. View of the stripped area (see Fig. 52) during the process of excavation. This is probably the most important part of the settlement area in Roztoky where its early medieval history may have begun: there is a cluster of three residential buildings of unusual size and plan and a sacrificial pit (centre right).

57. The same place a year later. As seen the destructive effects pass quite quickly but all the features are still recognisable.

58/1–4. Sunken houses of rectangular plan are the most common features which have been found in the early medieval settlement area at Roztoky. The third figure shows the plan of two superimposed buildings each of which had a north-west stone heating facility, and the upper one (1038) a set of four pottery vessels.

1037 · 1037 A · 1038/2

0 1m

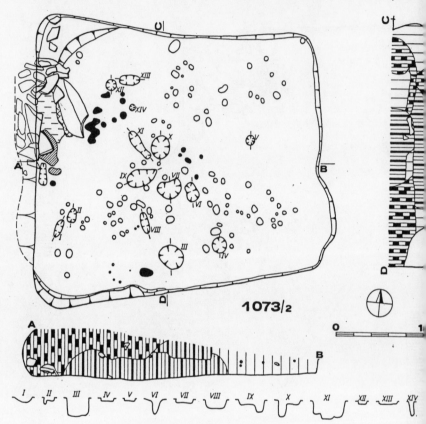

1073/2

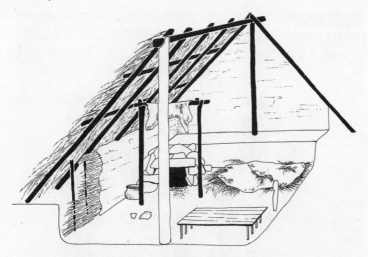

59. Reconstruction of an early medieval one-room sunken-floored hut from Roztoky.

and thirteen features). The huts are situated in two or three rows along a slope perpendicular to the contour line.

The fact that some of the sub-sites were settled repeatedly is evidenced by the superimposition of two or three features. The fundamental question of the interpretation of the whole area is thus the number of hamlets coexisting in a single chronological stage or phase. The experience obtained and published up to now, the extension of the whole area (that is, of the assumed agricultural appurtenances), and the general character of the natural conditions permit the conclusion that the image obtained by excavations would imply a small number of basic social units, that is one or two groups with between four and ten families, inhabiting short-term hamlets which frequently relocated.

Up to now some 110 typical features – huts – of the Early Slavic period have been found. These are sunken-floored habitation facilities called, in terms of the present terminology, mostly *Grubenhäuser* or pithouses (known as sunken-featured buildings in Britain). The floors were mostly sunk some 70–100 centimetres below the surface. The oblongs of the ground plans of the sunken parts of these features closely approximate squares by the ratios of their longer and shorter sides; the respective side lengths usually vary around 350 × 300 centimetres (border values:

60/1–3. Stone ovens were of various sizes and constructions.

260 × 240 and 420 × 400 centimetres). The basic construction elements of the surface parts of the shelters are large post-holes, which held the axial posts supporting the ridge-poles of the roofs. Larger post-holes in the corners or in the remaining areas and a shallow trench for a wooden beam which turn up here and there may be interpreted as further construction elements.

The most typical elements of the interior furnishing of the residential units were heating facilities (ovens, hearths). All of these were situated in corners, mostly north-western ones, and built of flat slabs of the local schist. The ovens consisted of several layers of these and the top parts were covered by slabs laid horizontally in the fashion of a primitive vault. In a few cases, another fireplace – a simple hearth – has been documented. Feature 739 had another closed heating facility, a vaulted clay oven (vaulting preserved) sunk into the hut wall at the side of the stone-built oven.

The standard interior furnishing included pottery vessels permanently sunk into floors in close proximity to the stone heating facilities. These had obviously served as water containers or for storage of foodstuffs (flour or grain).

Pits in walls and floors at the corners of some pithouses might have served as food cellars. These were circular spaces, sections of which measured 30–60 centimetres below the level of the hut

61/1–2. In a limited number of cases one ceramic vessel or a set, situated next to a heating facility (stone oven), were uncovered.

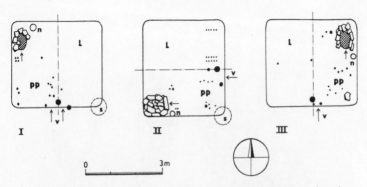

62. Types of possible spatial arrangement of the Roztoky houses based on evidence of living activity: n = pottery vessel; s = cellar; v = entrance; L = place for bed; PP = working area (after M. Gojda – M. Kuna).

63. A sacrificial pit found in Roztoky was full of quarry stones. At the bottom a cow's skull and an earthen ladle lying bottom-up were uncovered.

64. Two examples of the typical C6–7 hand-made pottery. Only rarely are preserved pots found on prehistoric habitation sites. Roztoky is exceptional since its collection amounts to more than twenty of them.

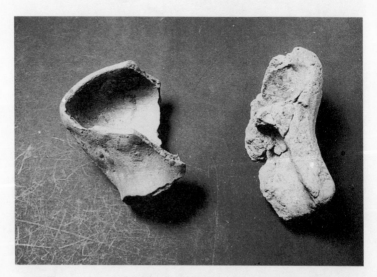

65. Two earthern ladles from Roztoky: the left one (a fragment) was used for pouring tin solder, the right one was found in the sacrificial pit.

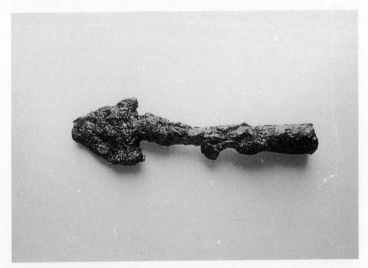

66. Iron spear-head.

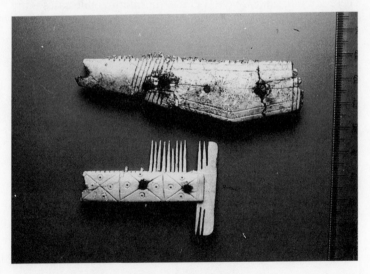

67. One- and two-sided combs made of bone.

floor. Further evidence of the interior furnishings and equipment of early Slavic huts is provided by a small peg holes which occurred frequently in some cases but in minimum numbers elsewhere. Groups of such holes in front of the orifice of the oven heating space, occurring repeatedly, may attest to the construction of two posts repeated several times and bearing either a smoke-evacuation device or perches for drying foods.

The spatial arrangement of the interior of the residential structures represents a constantly recurring scheme. If the oven is located in the NW sector, as in most cases, the oven gate opens into the SW sector with the densest clustering of peg holes – a work area. The peg holes may 'spill over' into the adjacent SE sector – a supplementary work area, the assumed 'holy corner'. The emptiest is the NE sector at the side of the oven; the bed might well have been located there. Food cellars, in so far as the huts have them, are situated in SW or SE corners. Post-holes for the roof-carrying beams are always situated at the sides opposing those with ovens, at the sides towards which the oven gates open. These are hut sides which – at least in interpretable cases – are turned towards the centre of the settlement cluster. Entrances into the buildings must be assumed in southern gable walls; it is rather unlikely that entrances would have been placed at the rear sides of huts through the sleeping quarters. If the oven is situated in the SW sector the whole scheme is merely turned through 90° with the entrance eastwards. Location of the oven in the NE hut corner implies reversal of the sides of the whole scheme while the north–south orientation of the hut is adhered to.

Economic facilities include pits for food storage (grain). They were most densely clustered in the northernmost part of the area, situated next to individual houses in groups of three. They are cylindrical or pear-shaped, reaching depths of 80–180 centimetres.

Most of the pottery found in individual features represent simple hand-made vase-shaped vessels. Only a fraction of the pottery production is decorated by multiple horizontal or wavy incised lines, stamps or raised ribs.

Apart from the pottery, other items of material culture from the site of Roztoky include articles of attire (an iron belt buckle), brass mounting, fragments of silver ornamented plate, glass beads, tools and objects of daily use (knives), a firesteel, quern-

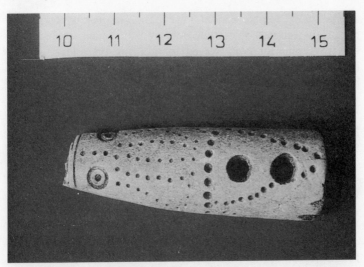

68. Fragment of a bone find, probably a whistle.

69. Cooperation between the Czech and British archaeologists in progress: a group of students from the York University's Department of Archaeology helping to excavate the site of Roztoky in summer 1989.

stones, bone combs, etc. and weapons (an iron arrow). One important find was an earthen pouring ladle which, according to spectrographic analysis, served for pouring tin solder. This is direct evidence for metal manufacture, at least for smithing purposes, on the site. Another earthen ladle, but of different shape, comes from a pit which has been interpreted as a sacrificial feature – a cow skull buried under massive slabs of stone in a pear-shaped pit. The significance of this feature for the whole settlement area's chronology is enormous since it probably indicates its first stage.

The excavations at Roztoky unearthed a settlement area of unprecedented density, the largest concentration of settlement vestiges of the C6–7 AD in Central Europe, the territory of Western Slavs. The excavations have revealed a number of questions pertaining both to the settlement topography of the Prague region of those times and to the character of the economic resources and the hinterland of early medieval rural communities. Two facts merit attention here: the existence of frequent early Slavic settlements in the site's vicinity (Bohnice-Zámka, Brnky, Čimice) and the absence, in the total area of Roztoky, of later settlements which would correspond to Slavic finds in the left-bank region north-west of Prague as evidence of the economic hinterland of such important local sites as the hillforts of Levý Hradec and Budeč.

6

Old-Slavic settlement investigation and its future directions

Expansion is the process that usually follows the final stage of ethnogenetical evolution. In the case of the Slavs this process was influenced by external conditions. In C5–6 Europe witnessed extensive transfers of various tribes that gave the name to those times: the Migration period. These events were affected drastically by ethnic groups unknown by that time, the Slavs. Their number and the power through which they occupied south-east and central Europe alarmed their contemporaries and squeezed the then rulers, especially the Byzantine emperors. Their raids were different from those carried out by nomadic groups from the East (which were repeated frequently) because the new population settled permanently in the colonised territories and did not return to their original territory in the East.

The settlement process of the Slavs was, on the one hand, influenced by many factors impinging from outside and, on the other hand, was determined by internal socio-economic development. At any rate it definitely influenced history.

There are many disciplines through which to analyse the settlement process of the ancient Slavs. Each of them has its own methods and approaches. It is archaeology and linguistics that are the most important branches in searching for the origins of the Slavs (since other historical sources are almost absent), while other disciplines are involved in the study of later history (the state-forming process, cultural development, etc.) of Slavic territorial units that were constituted after the Great Expansion.

External manifestations of an ethnohistorical process are, of course, varied. Material culture is for us, in the early medieval period, still the primary source of information and must be considered as such. The contradiction between the right evaluation of a site, feature and object, and their original function, is the basic problem which recently has been taken into account. It is difficult to assess the extent to which we are able to decipher an archaeological source. The difficulty consists especially in the fact that each archaeological source is just a fragmentary remain which was an integral part of a wide context within which it may have functioned differently from how we imagine. Another problem follows on from that one, namely whether the original context in which a feature or object operated is or is not preserved in the find context (or, in other words, whether the find context corresponds to the original one). Archaeology seeks for means of minimising the disjunction between 'how it really was' and 'how we find it': to find history we must learn to pick up single components and attribute the right meaning and function to them. This is the basis for successful archaeological interpretation that serves as the starting point to an historical synthesis.

At present it is the complex (or total, holistic) approach toward settlement study that is preferred. This does not mean that we focus exclusively upon the whole. The point is that the role and position of a structure's components may be grasped better if considered from the angle of the whole system within which it operates and of which it is an integral part. From the methodological viewpoint this means that preference is given to the deductive, rather than the inductive approach. In this sense archaeology of the medieval period co-operates closely with other disciplines, especially geography. As an expression of this symbiosis a special branch – settlement geography – has been constituted. Apart from archaeology and physical geography it is engaged also in the study of place-names, church dedications, art history, etc.

The multi-disciplinary approach has recently been adopted in those countries which traditionally have a reputation for archaeological research. There are wide variations, not only in financial conditions and field technology, but also in the quality of leadership. Considering that the present landscape changes radically and that, implicitly, its original appearance disappears step by step through the progress of civilisation, the choosing of the right research strategy must be our primary goal. This means that archaeology must focus on the careful co-ordination of research and rescue excavations and on the survey of those landscape units which still contain the residua of their prehistoric (or medieval) character – densely populated in centuries gone by but endangered by the future activity of present society. By the mobilisation of all possible means we have a chance to find at least some basic models of prehistoric and medieval settlement and some regularities in mutual relations amongst single communities, and to appreciate their dependence on the landscape types. We should try to decipher the principal laws governing the creation of the cultural landscape in history and to apply this information to the evolution of modern trends in the relations between Man and Nature. Thus, the study of history becomes meaningful.

SELECT BIBLIOGRAPHY

Angelov, D. 1980: *Die Entstehung des bulgarischen Volkes*. Berlin.

Beranová, M. 1986: 'Types of Slavic agricultural production in the 6th–12th centuries AD', *Ethnologia Slavica*, 16, pp. 7–48. Bratislava.

Beranová, M. 1988: *Slované*. Prague.

Biddle, M. 1976: 'Towns' in: *The archaeology of Anglo-Saxon England*, ed. D. Wilson, pp. 99–150. London.

Comşa, M. 1960: 'La pénetration des Slaves dans le territoire de la Roumanie entre VIème et IXème siècle à la lumière des recherches archéologiques, *Slavia Antiqua*, 7.

Dějiny hmotné kultury I/1, ed. J. Petráň. Prague, 1985.

Descriptio civitatum et regionum ad septentrionalem plagam Danubii, ed. B. Horák and D. Trávníček. Prague, 1956.

Die Slawen in Deutschland. Geschichte und Kultur der slawischen Stämme westlich von Oder und Niesse vom 6. bis 12. Jahrhundert. Ein Handbuch. Berlin (2nd edition) 1985.

Donat, P. 1980: *Haus, Hof and Dorf in Mitteleuropa von 7. – 12. Jahrhundert*. Berlin.

Dvorník, F. 1956: *The Slavs*. Boston.

Gimbutas, M. 1971: *The Slavs*. London.

Gojda, M. 1988: *The development of the settlement pattern in the basin of the lower Vltava (Central Bohemia) 200–1200*. BAR International Series 447. Oxford.

Gojda, M. 1990: 'The Czech and British medieval rural settlement studies: towards whole landscapes' in: *From the Baltic to the Black Sea: studies in medieval archaeology*, ed. D. Austin and L. Alcock. London.

Gojda, M. and Kuna, M. 1986: 'Roztoky – a newly discovered settlement area of the early Slavic period' in: *Archaeology in Bohemia 1981–1985*, pp. 175–82. Prague.

Hensel, W. 1965: *Die Slawen im frühenMittelalter*. Berlin.

Hensel, W. 1974: *Ur – und Frühgeschichte Polens*. Berlin.

Herrmann, J. 1966: *Tornow und Vorberg*. Berlin.

Herrmann, J. 1971: *Zwischen Hradschin und Vineta*. Leipzig–Jena–Berlin.

Justová, J. 1981: 'Slavic settlement at the site of Staré Badry by Opolánky' in: *Nouvelles Archéologiques dans la République socialiste Tchèque*, pp. 164–5. Prague–Brno.

Justová, J. 1986: 'Libice – a centre of the eastern domain of Bohemia. Excavations of the bailey' in: *Archaeology in Bohemia 1981–1985*, pp. 191–8. Prague.

Karger, M.K. 1958, 1961: *Drevnij Kijev I–II*. Moscow–Leningrad.

Karger, M.K. 1961: *Novgorod Velikij*. Moscow–Leningrad.

Klanica, Z. 1986: *Počátky slovanského osídleni našich zemí. Die Anfänge der slawischen Besiedlung unserer Ländern*. Prague.

Klápště, J. and Smetánka, Z. 1982: 'Archeologický výzkum české středověké vesnice v letech 1971–1981. Archäologische Untersuchungen mittelalterlicher Dörfer Böhmens in den Jahren 1971–1981' in: *Archaeologia Historica*, 7, pp. 11–31. Brno.

Klápště, J. and Smetánka, Z. 1986: 'Studies of the structure of medieval settlement of Bohemia' in *Archaeology in Bohemia 1981–1985*, pp. 247–52. Prague.

Krüger, B. 1967: *Dessau-Mosigkau, ein frühslawischer Siedlungsplatz in mittleren Elbegebiet*. Berlin.

Kudrnáč, J. 1970: *Klučov. Staroslovanské hradiště ve středních Čechách. Klučov. Ein altslawischer Burgwälle in Bohmen*. Prague.

Kurnatowska, Z. 1977: *Słowiańszczyzna południowa*. Wrocław–Warsaw–Kraków–Gdańsk.

Leciejewicz, L. 1976: *Słowiańszczyzna zachodnia*. Wrocław–Warsaw–Kraków–Gdańsk.

Łowmiański, H. 1963–73: *Początky Polski. Z dziejów Słowian w I tysiącleciu n.e. I–V*. Warsaw.

Nekuda, V. 1975: *Pfaffenschlag. Zaniklá středověká ves u Slavonic*. Brno.

Nekuda, V. 1982: 'Středověká vesnice na Moravě ve světle archeologických výzkumů zaniklých osad. Das mittelalterliche Dorf in Mähren' in: *Archaeologia Historica*, 7, pp. 33–66.

Niederle, L. 1923, 1926: *Manuel de l'antiquité slave I–II*. Paris.

Pleinerová, I. 1975: *Březno, vesnice prvních Slovanů v severozápadních Čechách. Březno, ein Dorf der frühesten Slawen in Nordwestböhmen*. Prague.

Pleinerová, I. 1986: 'Archaeological experiments at Březno. Building Slavic huts and living in them' in: *Archaeology in Bohemia 1981–1985*, pp. 289–300. Prague.

Schuldt, E. 1962: *Slawische Burgen in Mecklenburg*. Schwerin.

Sedov, V.V. 1979: *Proischožděnije i rannaja istoria slavjan*. Moscow.

Sklenář, K. 1983: *Archaeology in Central Europe: the first five hundred years*. Leicester–New York.

Sláma, J. 1983: 'Přínos archeologie k poznání počátků přemyslovského státu. Beitrag der Archäologie zur Kenntniss der Anfänge des

Přemyslidenstaates' in: *Acta Musei Nationalis Pragae*, Vol. XXXVII/2–3, pp. 159–69.

Sláma, J. 1986: 'Střední Čechy v raném středověku II. Hradiště, příspěvky k jejich dějinám a významu. Mittelböhmen im frühen Mittelalter II. Die Burgwälle, Beitrage zu ihrer Geschichte und Bedeutung' *Praehistorica*, XI. Prague.

Sláma, J. 1988: Střední Čechy v raném středověku III. Archeologie o počátcích přemyslovského státu. Central Bohemia in the Early Middle Ages III. Archaeology and the beginnings of the Přemysl-dynasty state. Praehistorica XIV. Praha. Prague.

Slownik Starożytności Słowiańskich. Wrocław–Warsaw–Kraków–Gdańsk, 1961 et seq.

Smetánka, Z. 1988: *Život středověké vesnice. Zaniklá Svídna. The life of a medieval village. The deserted village of Svídna*. Prague.

Snášil, R. 1971: 'Záblacany (okres Uherské Hradiště). Záblacany (Bezirk Uherské Hradiště)' in: *Zaniklé středověké vesnice v ČSSR ve světle archeologických výzkumů/Mittelalterliche Dorfwüstungen in der ČSSR im Lichte archäologischer Grabungen*, pp. 89–116. Uherské Hradiště.

Stančev, S. 1966: *Veliki Preslav*. Sofia.

Szymański, W. 1973: *Słowiańszczyzna wschodnia*. Wrocław–Warsaw–Kraków–Gdańsk.

Šolle, M. 1966: *Stará Kouřim a projevy velkomoravské hmotné kultury v Čechách. Alt Kouřim und die grossmährische Kultur in Böhmen*. Prague.

Šolle, M. 1984: *Staroslovanské hradisko*. Prague.

Váňa, Z. 1970: *Einführung in die Frühgeschichte der Slawen*. Neumünster.

Váňa, Z. 1980: 'Poznámky k etnogenezi a diferenciaci Slovanů z hlediska poznatků archeologie a jazykovědy. Betrachtungen zur ethnogenese und Differenzierung der Slawen', *Památky archeologické*, pp. 225–37.

Váňa, Z. 1983: *The world of the ancient Slavs*. London–Detroit.

Váňa, Z. 1986: 'Budeč – a ducal residence in the centre of Bohemia according to excavations in the latest years' in: *Archaeology in Bohemia 1981–1985*, pp. 191–8. Prague.

Zeman, J. 1966: 'Zu den chronologischen Fragen der ältesten slawischen Besiedlung im Bereich der Tschechoslowakei', *Archeologické rozhledy*, 18, 157–89.

Zeman, J. 1976: 'Nejstarší slovanské osídlení Čech./Die älteste slawische Besiedlung Böhmens', *Památky archeologické*, LXVII, pp. 115–235.

Zeman, J. and Buchvaldek, M. 1967: 'Sídlištní nálezy ze starší doby hradištní ve Vřesníku', *Památky archeologické*, LVIII, pp. 545–62.

Index